MOOSE HEADS ON THE TABLE

KARIN TENELIUS AND LISA GILL

MOOSE HEADS ON THE TABLE

Stories about self-managing organisations from Sweden

tuffleadershiptraining

http://www.tuffleadershiptraining.com

ISBN 978-91-519-5450-9

Book cover and illustrations by Sophie Wainwright.

Printed by: BOD, Germany 2020

'Go to the people. Live with them. Learn from them. Love them. Start with what they know. Build with what they have. But with the best leaders, when the work is done, the task accomplished, the people will say: "We have done this ourselves."'

Lao Tzu, Tao Te Ching

Content

Introduction

By Lisa Gill

When my colleague and co-author, Karin Tenelius, first began talking at conferences back in the nineties about her experiences of transforming companies into 'bottom-up' organisations without managers, she was met with total scepticism, amusement and even outrage. So much so that she eventually gave up and vowed not to speak publicly about this topic until Sweden, and the world, was ready. At the time of writing this book, things have certainly shifted. We still have a long way to go, of course, but more and more people are practicing in, and researching and writing about, self-managing organisations. More evidence is emerging about the benefits of working in decentralised ways: agility, responsiveness, rehumanising workplaces, collective intelligence, enhanced responsibility, exceptional service – the list goes on. The case no longer needs to be made for reinventing our management models.

For Karin and me, the motivation for contributing to the field of self-managing organisations is twofold. Firstly, we want to help create more human workplaces. Organisations where people can draw on their full intelligence, creativity, and responsibility to do great work together and grow as individuals. Secondly, research and theory is one thing, but practice is something else entirely. The stories in this book are born out of experimentation, trial and error, and lots of practice. We want to embolden others to do the same.

How this book began

Karin and I met in January 2016 in Cascais, Portugal. We, along with nine other strangers, had been called there by a passionate Spanish woman called Dunia Reverter to explore the idea of setting up a company that would buy and transform other companies. A common thread for many of us was an enthusiasm for the book *Reinventing Organisations* by Frederic Laloux, which had been published two years earlier. Dunia had explained to me on Skype: 'If we wait for the CEOs and founders to become 'enlightened', it's gonna take forever! We need to buy and transform companies! That's how we accelerate this paradigm shift! So, I'm inviting a bunch of people to my house in Cascais to explore this. Are you in?' Of course I said yes.

Karin and Dunia had been connected by Jos de Blok, the founder of a large self-managing nursing organisation in the Netherlands called Buurtzorg, after Dunia had shared her plan with him at a conference he was speaking at. 'You want to buy and transform companies? You need to talk to Karin Tenelius,' he told her, 'we met the other day and she's been doing exactly that as far back as the nineties!'

I'm profoundly grateful to Dunia for enabling Karin and I to meet. It was in Cascais that I first heard some of Karin's stories about organisations she had transformed. At the time, I had been focusing on changing the structures and processes in organisations in my coaching and consulting work, and was convinced that once you did this, everything else would follow. But Karin had not transformed these organisations by changing the machinery of them, she had done it in an entirely human way – through dialogues. She spoke of giving away the authority to the team, coaching people to take full responsibility for the business, and supporting them to have radically honest conversations. It struck me, then, that we need to go beyond structures and processes to what Otto Scharmer calls our blind spot – the place from which we're operating. Our worldview, our mindset, our way of being, how we relate to each other. All of these things are at the heart of the transformation that needs to happen in each of us if we want our organisations to really shift. It's these stories that Karin and I wanted to share. She had been waiting for the right time to share them and the right person to help her tell them.

We've been writing this book together over the course of nearly three years, during which time I've become part of the team at Tuff Leadership Training, the company Karin co-founded to train managers in more traditionally structured companies the very skills she had discovered were so powerful in a self-managing organisation – how to unleash the potential in others through coaching, adult-to-adult dialogues.

In recent years, more and more companies have begun to partner with Tuff to guide them on their journey to becoming a self-managing organisation. What used to be a radical idea met with scepticism, even in 'progressive' Sweden, is now becoming more widely understood as a way to create organisations that are much more adaptive and resilient in contexts of complexity. We believe self-managing organisations, those that radically decentralise authority, tap into the full potential of capable adults and generate totally new levels of cooperation, communication, responsibility, commitment and creativity.

But self-management is hard!

We have so many conversations with people who are committed to another way of working but are struggling with meaty challenges like: How can we create a culture of accountability in a self-managing organisation? What does leadership look like in a company where there are no bosses? How do we make decisions effectively? How do we foster a culture that will allow our self-managing organisation to thrive? What do self-set salaries look like? How do we have tough conversations? Where do we start? What mindset shift is required?

In this book we'll share our thoughts and experiences regarding these questions, although we make no claims of having all the answers. There is no one right way to do this. There are some common principles and practices that are useful, but we believe every organisation needs to find their own way.

The purpose of this book

The purpose of this book is to support people in putting self-managing organisations and teams into practice. Karin has spent nearly twenty years experimenting and developing an approach to self-managing teams based on training people in a coaching leadership style and building their capacity to communicate at a deeper level to foster true collaboration.

However, we've consciously chosen not to write a handbook for three reasons; (1) every organisation is different and therefore there is no linear process to teach, (2) mindset and skills are almost impossible to learn by reading, it requires experiencing, and (3) we want to encourage readers to take what they find useful and then find their own way of transforming or developing their teams.

At the core of this book are stories about a number of small Swedish companies across different sectors that Karin helped transform, both as an owner and as a consultant or interim CEO. In these stories are insights and lessons we want to share, coupled with some of the ground principles that underpin them. We will share the beautiful triumphs Karin and these teams experienced, as well as the painful failures and lessons learned.

Changing systems is not enough

Our biggest motivation for writing this book is that we would like to contribute to this field by offering a perspective that is grounded not in structures and processes, but in ways of being and mindset. We find there is less written and shared about the latter, and yet if we really want to shift our organisations, we have to go deeper. As Simon Mont wrote in his article 'Autopsy of a Failed Holacracy: Lessons in Justice, Equity, and Self-Management' for the *Nonprofit Quarterly*:

> Shifting into a new formal structure is in many ways the easy part, because it's the most visible – the easiest to put our hands

on and tinker with. The real work comes when we have to relearn how to relate on personal and interpersonal levels and look at the project of self-governance in the context of our full human lives.

Towards the end of writing this book, I interviewed the international Nonviolent Communication teacher and author Miki Kashtan for our podcast, Leadermorphosis, and she poignantly shared the three places shifts need to occur in order for organisational self-management to thrive. First, those who have (or have had) structural power (for instance, former managers) need to learn how to distribute it and unlearn their 'top-down' tendencies towards others. Second, those who didn't or don't have structural power need to learn how to step into their own leadership, to ask for what they need, to take the initiative to identify challenges and opportunities – which in some ways is much harder because it incurs more of an interpersonal risk, especially if those mentioned in the first shift aren't doing so well. And finally, we need to reinvent our structures and systems – otherwise we just inherit the old ones.

We hope that this book can contribute towards a deeper understanding of the first two shifts Miki mentions, the ones that concern our way of relating to each other as human beings. At the core of the approach Karin has developed over the years to support organisations to become self-managing are three pillars: 1) a coaching leadership mindset and way of being, 2) a focus on working climate, and 3) a culture of mandate and involvement. All of these are fostered through new kinds of facilitated dialogues that build human capacities for working together in radically different ways.

Whether you are starting from scratch, using or customising a pre-designed self-management system like Holacracy or Sociocracy, or have home-grown your own approach to organisational self-management, we believe these pages can offer you some value and complement what's already in place.

Our invitation

We believe that you don't have to know everything about self-management to start the journey. You can start from where you are and work with what you've got. And in the simplest terms, what you've got is your colleagues and fellow human beings. Karin developed the approach to organisational self-management you'll read about in this book through trial and error and lots of practice. We hope you will be emboldened to do the same. The invitation is to experiment, to learn by doing, to start with where you are and work with what you've got. And to keep practicing.

From the next chapter onwards, the book will be in Karin's voice. They are, after all, her stories. However, you'll notice pop-out boxes throughout the book that go into theory, tools or examples in more detail. These will be in my voice, and I'll talk about Karin in the third person. At the back of the book are some resources we've chosen to help you on your journey. It's not an exhaustive list but the purpose is to offer some starting points and insights that might support you.

Karin's stories

How I got here

Before I share the stories of the organisations I helped trans-form, let me briefly tell my own story and how I came to develop the dialogue-based approach to organisational self-management we will share in this book.

The first seed of interest in self-managing organisations (though we didn't use that term then) was when I was study-ing marketing in 1986 whilst working in the hotel industry in Sweden. As part of my studies, I read lots of books about service management. All of the books said the same thing: the degree to which employees are involved and given authority determines the quality of customer service. I read the former CEO of Scandinavian Airlines Jan Carlzon's book *Moments of Truth*, which was a revelation. But it was another book that would make an even bigger impression on me: Ricardo Semler's *Maverick*. Here was a man who had inherited his father's traditionally-run company, Semco corporation, and transformed it into a democratic organisation by removing management layers and giving employees a say in how the business was run – and with wild success! I wanted a piece of this.

At the end of the eighties, the Swedish economy was booming. For me this meant a new job as a marketing director in a large corporation in the education sector. When I started, there were two visionary leaders on the management team who gave me a lot of space to change the company's old fashioned ways. To my surprise, I also inherited a team of four people who were equally enthusiastic, and knowledgeable, about these ideas of involving employees and giving them more authority. Together we started a big change project which involved a roadshow to meet employees in office all across the country. We were halfway through the project and enjoying lots of quality discussions when suddenly the two visionary senior managers left the company and were replaced by a more traditional CEO. The project was halted and I was confronted by the slow, top-down style of management that I now know to be commonplace in the corporate world. Fed up with the constraints of the corporate world, I left at age 29 to start my own business. That marketing role would be my last proper job.

Transformation through dialogues

At this point, a friend of mine had attended a personal development course and I had noticed a huge change in her. I had never done anything like that but, curious to know more, I signed up. Over the course of the training, I had two significant insights. The first was I discovered the transformative power when we human beings are able to shift our mindset. Rather than external factors or what we *do*, I realised that how we *relate* to things profoundly influences our way of being and therefore the results we get. Like wearing a pair of coloured glasses, our mindset colours everything we experience. If we change the glasses, we change how things occur to us and therefore open up a whole other world of possibility.

The second insight I got was that I noticed something the trainers did at the beginning of the course involving a contract between trainers and participants. To everyone else, it seemed like tedious admin but I saw how it was vitally important to creating accountability amongst the participants and inviting them to own their own learning outcomes. In the years that followed when I was working as a freelance consultant, I began to use this contracting technique in the service and leadership training I delivered.

Then in the nineties there was a big recession in Sweden. I suddenly found myself coaching hundreds of unemployed job seekers, five years or so before the concept of coaching was known in Sweden. This gave me an excellent opportunity to practice what I had learned in the personal development course. I began to develop a method of coaching that weaved in the contracting technique I'd experienced and the ability to help people become aware of and shift their mindset. Over hundreds of sessions, I began to see real results. Later, in 2007, I published a book outlining the principles of this method called 'Arbetsmarknadscoaching,' which has now been widely adopted in Sweden. It was when I began to train others in this method that I realised the key is for the coach to have what I call a coaching, adult-to-adult mindset and way of being. (We'll explore this in more detail in Chapter 1.)

Finally, in the late nineties I was given an opportunity to

integrate all of these elements and experiment with what I then called 'bottom-up' organising, inspired by the likes of Ricardo Semler.

What if we discovered we were working too hard at transformation? That we could do much less and get powerful results, and fast?

Imagine you're in a room full of people who have been unemployed for years and who have just rated their chances of getting a job next to zero. Now imagine that, three to four hours later, they rate their chances of getting a job at 50% or more.

Picture a group of fifty employees around a board table, roaring with anger and shooting icy comments at each other, behaving more like hostile teenagers than professional adults. Would you think it possible that in just a few hours they could be transformed into a constructive and thoughtful group of human beings?

Or consider a rigid, hierarchical workplace where people have always been told what to do and have become passive, helpless victims, metamorphosing into an entrepreneurial, creative workforce taking responsibility for the whole company – in just six weeks.

I have witnessed remarkable transformations like these and all that's happened to catalyse the shift from one state to another is these people engaging in and participating in different dialogues. When I began to experiment with different dialogues early in my career, I saw I was able to create opportunities for groups and individuals to shift attitudes and mindsets in an instant. As my facilitation skills in leading these

kind of processes improved and developed, I began to realise
the incredible results that were possible in just a short space of
time. These are my stories.

Karin Tenelius

Part 1

Three case studies of transforming companies as a consultant or interim CEO

1. Freys Hotel: a successful hotel gets a surprise boost from self-management

'The real voyage of discovery consists not in seeking new lands but seeing with new eyes.'

Marcel Proust

In 1999 I was working as a freelance consultant taking on fairly traditional coaching and service training assignments when I was contacted by a friend of mine. Annika Tell was the manager of two small hotels in the centre of Stockholm called Freys Hotel and although the business was profitable and doing well, she was looking for something that would give the employees a bit of an energy injection. So one quiet Sunday in September I ran a standard, four-hour service training session. As I often did, I mentioned Ricardo Semler's book *Maverick* which I used to call 'the bible for the world's most unusual workplace.' At one point I asked the group, 'If you had the authority to make all these changes you're talking about, would you?' The room was silent. It was a magic moment because I could feel the energy in the room, just below the surface, ready to be awakened. Annika was intrigued and immediately went away and read *Maverick*, learning about how Semler had successfully transformed Semco through democratising its workforce and giving frontline employees more decision-making power. She came back to me, suddenly firing on all cylinders. 'Let's do it!' she said. I was excited. I saw this as my first real opportunity to put these ideas into practice and gather proof that it could really work. Annika is a wonder for putting ideas into action. She talked to the owner of the hotel and got carte blanche. It didn't take much for the hotel employees to be on board as Annika was well-liked and known for her confidence and creative ideas.

Lying in wait

The process began in September with me facilitating discussions with the team to explore what they needed and what was getting in their way to achieve this. We discovered, after some probing, that some people felt the culture wasn't as open as others did. I noticed that simply naming this and giving space for the group to reflect on this lack of openness actually resulted in people starting to talk more openly with each other. However, it was tentative and many others still seemed hesitant. Team meetings tended to be long and inefficient.

Before I had started working with them, the employees had designed a grand vision for the business. In all honesty, I felt a bit overwhelmed by it. Where should we start? But gradually, a path began to emerge. What unfolded was that the employees didn't trust that *they* were now in charge. Annika was very liked as a leader and seen as competent, charismatic, and full of ideas. However, this also meant that the team had been conditioned to await instructions and so had become passive, unable to direct themselves or their meetings. I decided to address this in two ways: one would be to coach Annika to be a more empowering leader and step back, and the other would be to coach the group to step into their new authority.

Pillar #1: A coaching mindset and way of being

If you are the founder, CEO, or a leader in your team or organisation, sorry but you are the biggest obstacle to your team's success! If the team senses in any way that you are still 'in charge,' your team will never reach their full potential. We have found that one of the essential pillars of an effective self-managing organisation is developing a coaching mindset and way of being. Though this idea is important for former managers, it's relevant to all individuals in a self-managing team as it helps build a culture of development more broadly.

Coaching is a term that's often misused or misunderstood so let's clarify what we mean by coaching. Here's the definition we use:

> The purpose of coaching is to empower another person to achieve their desired aim. Coaching is a 'way of being' which enables another person to choose to draw on their own potential.

Rather than an activity, we like to think of coaching as a way of being, one that you can embody in many different situations: in a project meeting, when a colleague asks for help, in a conversation with a client, or in a strategy discussion. It's a way of being that is both compassionate and tough, one that encourages an adult-to-adult, partnership dynamic. Have you ever had a manager or a colleague that brought out the best in

---

you just through their way of being? Without saying or doing anything, you just felt that this person believed in you and trusted you to do great work. When we are in the presence of these people, we become bigger versions of ourselves, and somehow we are able to achieve more than we ever thought possible. That phenomenon is what we call a coaching way of being.

Karin first developed a way of distinguishing this mindset and way of being when she was training job coaches to empower their clients, and later when she and her colleagues began to train managers all over the world in a coaching, adult-to-adult style of leadership. One way to characterise this mindset or way of being is through five cornerstones:

> **1. Relating to people's potential**
> **2. Placing responsibility with the group**
> **3. Clarifying and distinguishing**
> **4. Being able to be with it**
> **5. Not having your own (active) agenda**

Let's explore each one in a bit more detail.

Relating to people's potential

- Trust that the team has (or can have) the ability to:
  - Make a good decision
  - Take responsibility for generating ideas and solutions
  - Shift their working climate (more on this later)
  - Cope with adversities and complex challenges

Sounds obvious, doesn't it? But so often we human beings have a tendency to, often automatically and unconsciously, relate to a group or individual as not quite competent enough, or not fast enough, or not responsible enough. We might compensate for this by using our own strengths (at solving problems, for example) but in doing so, we rob them of opportunities to try and develop that capacity for themselves.

Or perhaps we're able to relate to people's potential when things are going well, but when they aren't, we find ourselves stepping in or being impatient. Or what about when a group appears to be totally passive or helpless or even useless? Then it can be almost impossible to relate to a group's potential. We can make all kinds of assumptions about why an individual or a group ends up in this state which then prevents us from relating to them as capable or adult or responsible. To really relate to people's potential is to trust that there is always potential there, even if it's not visible. Adopting a coaching mindset and way of being can help others (and ourselves) distinguish what is getting in the way in order for us to access our full potential or resources. Often, it's an unproductive mindset – that something is too risky or perhaps pointless, for example.

This being said, to relate to someone's potential doesn't mean we have to agree with everything they say, or listen to them complain endlessly, or expect that a miracle will happen. To relate to someone's potential is to truly believe that the person in front of us already has the capacity needed to achieve the seemingly impossible. Training and practicing as a coaching leader can help us relate to a person or a group's maximum potential, rather than their shortcomings. It involves talking adult-to-adult, not like a parent, a manager, or a do-gooder.

People can handle straight talking. Receiving frank feedback gives people the means to make a positive change. In order to develop, people need to acknowledge the different sides of their character. This doesn't mean there's something wrong with them, it just means that, like you and I, they have strengths and pitfalls.

Placing responsibility with the group

- Ensure that the team (and not the leader) is responsible for:
  - Solving problems
  - Leading and owning meetings
  - The company's results
  - The health of the team

If you are a manager, or someone in a role of perceived authority, people will have a tendency to heap their responsibilities onto you. Even if you are working in a self-managing organisation or team, we are so conditioned to working in subordinate ways in schools and workplaces that it's difficult to shift our mindset and behaviours to a new paradigm. As a leader, it's easy to fall into the trap of taking on this responsibility that is so readily offered, sometimes because we have a need to achieve or perform or help or take care of others.

At the same time, a self-managing organisation isn't about shunning leadership or power hierarchies. Many former leaders step back too far into abdication. Instead, it's important to allow people to step into their natural leadership – experience or expertise or energy. If you are someone with authority in the company, make sure you hand back all the responsibility that's not yours. This is less about what you do and more about how you are being. If your way of being is that you're responsible, your team members will never truly feel that they are responsible and it's likely they'll never fully tap into their potential as a result. And if you try to use the force of your will to get people onto the right track, or offer solutions, all you'll do is create resistance. It's everyone's duty to speak up if they notice someone hoarding responsibility or embodying a way of being that is coercive or top-down. When it happens, it's positive to name it, apologise, and move forward.

Clarifying and distinguishing
- Instead of advising or 'adding':
    - Reflect or mirror back to the group what you notice
    - Summarise themes and patterns
    - Name the climate or what's happening 'beneath the surface' in the group
    - State the group's current position or status in relation to a purpose or goal
    - Ask coaching questions

This is a valuable mindset and way of being for anyone to develop in order to contribute to a group. Again, it's especially important if you're someone with authority as we often have an automatic habit of giving advice or solutions, which can result in the group making themselves small or prevent them from accessing their own leadership. Of course, if people ask you for advice and it's appropriate for you to share it (*i.e.* you have experience or expertise), you can choose to give it. But it's a choice rather than a default mode of operating.

The clarifying and distinguishing cornerstone is about being a catalyst, bringing issues to the surface, creating a shared picture of the situation and raising awareness. When you learn to clarify and distinguish rather than jumping in with your own solutions, you release a huge amount of creativity and acceptance of responsibility in others.

Being able to be with it

- A state of being which is:
  - Being with things as they are without judgment
  - Permitting and accepting
  - Present and patient (not trying to change it or 'advance')

In Swedish there is a phrase for this: *gilla läget*, which literally means 'liking how it is.' This is about freeing ourselves up from thinking in terms of right and wrong and keeping our views and values in check in order to be a good coaching leader. It's a matter of meeting people on their own terms, accepting their attitude and behaviour without reacting to it. In other words, just be with it. It might feel counterintuitive, but in being this way, we contribute to achieving change. We can never create a shift in someone else, they have to use their own power to create a shift and that can only happen if we accept things are they are.

Sometimes we can fall into the trap of trying to cheer someone up or giving a pep talk to make things pleasant or more energetic. But when we do this, we become responsible for the group again. Having said this, being able to be with something doesn't mean that you give up or allow things to fail spectacularly. It's about a way of being. When we're triggered by something, we become reactive and therefore unable to contribute in a productive way. Being with it means accepting things as they are and from here, we can make observations and ask questions to help move things forward. It's a mindset shift from 'it shouldn't be like this' to 'ok, this is how it is right now.' If you notice a climate of resignation in the team, for example, that is how it is – right or wrong. It's how you relate to it that matters. You can address it but then give the team the responsibility of doing something about it.

Not your own (active) agenda

- A way of being where the agenda (purpose) of conversations is transparent and as involving as possible

In traditional, top-down organisations, we often have an agenda as managers which we impose on people, either transparently or coercively. In a self-managing organisation, it's good for people in leadership roles to allow the team's ambitions and purposes to steer conversations, even if we might have great plans and ideas ourselves. We act as a catalyst for others to achieve their goals. If we want people to take responsibility and initiative, they have to do it in line with a goal or interest or purpose of their own. When we have an unconscious plan or agenda for the other person in mind, it pollutes our way of being, our behaviours and therefore the result – people can smell it a mile away.

The red thread in all of these cornerstones is the ability to listen so that the other person feels truly heard and 'felt.' All (or nearly all) of our questions should come from our listening and not from our thinking or preconceived ideas. (We'll talk more about the importance of listening in Chapter 6.)

Working on your leadership pitfalls

If you're interested in developing your leadership skills, we've provided a table in the appendix to help you identify which of the cornerstones are your main development areas.

Together Annika and I discovered her biggest challenge was to trust that things would get done. She was a perfectionist and so in the beginning it was really difficult for her when she saw things weren't exactly how she wanted. I remember on one occasion her swallowing the urge to control when she noticed cigarette butts on the ground outside the entrance. I coached her through challenges like this, supporting her to pinpoint her pitfalls and how they were hindering others to step in and grow. For those of us who are or have been managers, we've usually built successful careers on certain qualities that can actually end up working against us when applied to the context of a self-managing team. For Annika, her great strengths of being a driven and creative manager meant she also had a tendency to be impatient and overly responsible. As time went on, she was able to choose to let this go. In the past, she would react to a situation lightning fast and rush in to correct it. Now she could choose to slow down and initiate dialogues with her teammates, something that took great courage and built real trust. In fact, becoming less involved in the day-to-day operations opened up space for her to work part-time as a therapist, something she found hugely rewarding.

Stepping into new-found authority

Back in the team, I decided that rather than pep talk them into action, I would confront them with their passiveness. I gave them some frank feedback and said, 'I experience you as being very quiet and disengaged. There's a lot of waiting and observing. It's like you're not responsible for this hotel.' I simply named this, without judging it, and was silent. Eventually, people began to speak up and reflect on my feedback. They realised they didn't have to wait for permission – they could choose to take charge right now! From that point on, they really engaged and started to act with their new-found authority. They decided to divide themselves into subgroups responsible for different parts of the vision, like 'Success Group' and 'Quality of Life Group.' I realised how important it was for me not to *add* anything or give advice, as this would make the group dependent on me. This would become a principle to live by in the other organisations I worked with, simply to distinguish the current status of the group and put it up on the table, so to speak, for the team to deal with. It was as if I had held a mirror up to the group and it suddenly dawned on them that the only thing stopping them was themselves.

Stages of group development

Looking back, I can see now that this initial phase of tentativeness was simply the first phase of the team's development. According to Will Schutz's FIRO Theory, teams go through three stages of development. The first is Inclusion, which is all about being quiet, observing, and deciding if you want to participate in this, trying to find who you are in this. The second phase is Control, which is where you start to try out and step into different roles. Conflicts also start to emerge in this phase. If a team can deal with and go through conflicts together, they reach the final stage, Openness. This is a stage of productivity, creativity, acceptance, and effectiveness. Ideally you want teams to go back and forth between stages as they develop further and circumstances change. Many teams never reach the Openness stage, which for me is the Holy Grail of collaboration.

At Freys Hotel, the Control phase happened about three or four months after I began coaching the group. One challenge that arose was two women in the group who began to emerge as manager types. With their newly discovered ability to address such issues, the team called attention to this. One of the women was really angry: 'It's really challenging when people around me don't take responsibility! It means I tend to do it all myself and then I feel overburdened.' Others in the team shared how sad they felt when they could see they were falling back into the old habit of someone else deciding for them and losing their freedom. The two women began to see that they needed to work on their 'big sister' tendencies, and their impatience for things to be done immediately. They were able to accept that everyone is different.

As a result of this meeting, the team realised they needed to make some agreements. Together they surfaced a couple of rules that they thought were useful and decided to commit to them. Some of the rules were things like: 'Attending meetings isn't mandatory – you're responsible for seeking out the information you need,' and 'It's important to be able to apologise,' and 'Do what you promised, or ask someone else to help.' For me this was a great indicator that the team was starting to develop an ability to maintain a productive working climate by being vigilant in noticing people's tendencies and raising issues that needed to be aired. They realised that they alone were responsible for their culture and their processes and if something wasn't working, they had to see how they could use discussions and agreements to clean it up.

As the months went on, I coached the team less and less as they became more self-sufficient. Rather than having a well-laid out plan, my coaching mostly consisted of sensing what was needed, asking tough questions, and giving the team plenty of honest feedback on what I was able to observe about the quality of their cooperation in order for them to develop further. One main focus was supporting them in mastering a decision making process that I learned from Will Schutz when I had trained to lead 'The Human Element' course called 'concordance.'

Insight #1: Concordance decision making

Concordance is a decision making method developed by American psychologist Will Schutz in the 1980s. He teaches us that in order to reach a concordant decision in a group, you need to create a safe space for people to express their feelings and develop adult to adult communication. Concordance is leagues away from traditional decision making, which tends to be based on talking, convincing, and arguing. Instead, concordance is about really listening to one another and being able to express our feelings, something that most professionals are not used to doing in the workplace.

How it works is that someone shares a proposal for a decision, and after asking clarifying questions, each person can share how they feel about the decision. The leader and the rest of the group's job then is not to defend or justify or convince, but to listen and perhaps ask clarifying questions. This is how Schutz describes the next part of the process in his book 'The Human Element':

> When a decision is about to be reached, if the leader says, 'Does anyone disagree?' and no one responds, it doesn't necessarily mean we have concordance. It may be that I don't feel comfortable expressing my disagreement, especially if we do not yet have an open atmosphere. One technique for getting the most honest and open participation, therefore coming closer to creating true concordance, is the 'Yes' method.
>
> After discussion of the issues, when we seem to understand where everyone stands, we phrase the question – in written form – and ask everyone to say the word yes if they agree or the word no if they disagree. We go all the way around the circle in turn, even if there is a no. The rule is, if anyone says anything other than a yes, we assume that he or she means no. If I feel reluctant to oppose the group, I often will not say no directly; I will express my lack of readiness implicitly, by saying yeah, sure, okay, go ahead, uh-huh, or something similar. Even a hesitant yes may mean a no. Encouraging me to say how I really feel leads to true concordance.
>
> If we have not all said the word yes, we continue the discussion until we either come to complete agreement or decide to postpone the decision. This does not mean we resort to compromise or averaging. It means we create a new formulation to the problem, so that the solution will satisfy everyone. One useful step is to ask dissenters, 'What would it take for you to be satisfied?' Creativity often emerges at this point.

You may be thinking at this point: 'This will take forever! We'll never get anything done!' But in our experience, once groups have practiced concordance decision making, they can become incredibly efficient at making decisions and the execution is much more effective because everyone has been heard and is satisfied with the proposal that's been decided on. Of course, we wouldn't recommend using concordance for every single decision. There are other decision-making methods that work well in self-managing organisations such as the advice process, consent-based decision methods, or using tools like Loomio. We recommend agreeing together which types of decision-making methods you want to use for different types of decisions. Concordance is particularly valuable for decisions that affect a large number of people or for which you want particularly strong engagement in order to make a smart decision and also to secure ownership of the final outcome.

The results

Just eight months after Annika and I had started our experiment with the team at Freys Hotel, the profit margin had increased by 26%. I believe the source of this result was two-fold. When employees develop a 'mental ownership' they start to see the business as theirs and act totally differently compared to a mindset of just 'clocking in.' If you see it as 'your' hotel, you want the hotel to be at 100% capacity every day, and you'll happily phone the booking agencies and offer any empty rooms if guests don't show or cancel or you aren't fully booked. When you have access to, and are involved in, the hotel's costs you start to relate to the money in a way that resembles how you look at your own household budget. Employees ask each other questions like: 'How could we cut down costs in this area without impacting the quality?' When a whole organisation starts to think and act in this way, it impacts the results. By the following year, profits had reached a record high. In April 2000, Annika wrote:

> Much has changed in the hotel. The engagement and care
> for the interior design and maintenance of the hotel is bigger
> than ever. The new working rota is the best I ever have seen.
> Someone has made an effort to find a new supplier of cleaning
> products. When another supplier didn't show up as promised,
> someone immediately phoned and complained. Mistakes aren't
> ignored the way they used to be. Things that need to be done
> happen much faster now. The self-esteem is visible because
> employees know what they want to see happen. The disorgan-
> ised feeling is gone. And we have only just begun ...'

43

There have also been two books written about Freys Hotel; one by Annika and another by the employees. The latter details in one chapter the process they went through to create a self-managed salary setting process which involved some difficult conversations, honest feedback, and a skilled execution of the concordant decision making method I had taught them.

What happened next?

I learned that a few years later, the team took a vote to decide if they still wanted to be self-managing since Annika had made the original decision and they really wanted to own this way of working. It was a unanimous 'yes,' which made me really happy. They continued to work in this way for some years. The business invested a lot in the personal development of the employees, sending them on 'The Human Element' trainings, for example. Sadly, nearly twenty years after we started this process, Annika has retired and the business seems to have reverted to traditional management again. It's always upsetting to see how quickly this way of working can unravel without someone to continue to hold the space for it.

Summary

- My work with Freys Hotel gave me a chance to see if it was possible to coach a team to become self-managing and achieve tangible business results in a short space of time. This example made it clear to me that when people began to regard a business as their own, they became, for example, better salespeople and started to think about how they could reduce unnecessary costs.

- I learned that declaring self-management isn't enough. Former managers need some coaching in unlearning their parent-like tendencies (like being overly-responsible) and employees often need some support in stepping into their new authority. Humans are, after all, creatures of habit.

- At the end of this process with Freys, I started to see the key pieces of a self-management transformational process – one of them being a coaching, adult-to-adult mindset and way of being.

2. Komanco: from chronic losses to big wins

> 'Leaders who don't learn to tell the weather themselves may unwittingly wind up with a warm and sunny forecast for what in reality is a cold and stormy company climate.'
>
> Hans W. Hagemann, *The Leading Brain*

Two years after my experience at Freys Hotel, I was on maternity leave after giving birth to my first son and itching for a new assignment. In February 2001, I met with Lars-Åke Almqvist, the vice president of one of Sweden's largest unions, overseeing staff in the country's 300 or so municipalities. He was also the founder and CEO of the union-owned consultancy that offered training for staff in the public sector. This company, called Komanco, was in crisis: it had never turned a profit and the organisation had been continually putting money in to cover the losses each year. In 2000, the accounts showed their biggest loss ever: 4.4 million SEK (around 480,000 Euros), the turnover at around 12–13 million Swedish Krona. Komanco was given an ultimatum – break even or close. I told Lars-Åke about the results we had achieved at Freys and proposed that I help develop Komanco into a self-managing organisation in a similar fashion. When he pitched it to the union board, they were extremely sceptical about the idea of trusting the employees with the fate of the company but they agreed to install me as CEO for eight months to see if we could try and turn the business around. I had some conditions, of course. I insisted that all employees had to say yes to me becoming CEO and the way that we would work together. I also was very clear that my intention was to take on no operational responsibilities whatsoever (indeed, I couldn't as my son was only two months old at this point), but rather to coach the team to become self-managing.

Breaking even at breakneck speed

On the 9th of March, I met with the fourteen consultants who worked at Komanco for an hour. I explained that this way of working involves everyone in the team taking collective responsibility for the business and that my only task as CEO is to coach the team. They were extremely enthusiastic about this approach, which wasn't surprising considering they were leadership consultants like me. Everyone knew in theory that when you involve employees, productivity and profitability go up, but I was sure to emphasise that it is quite a different thing in practice. I concluded the meeting by saying, 'if you choose to work with me as the CEO, each and every one of you also chooses to be responsible for the fate of this company. I won't bring any solutions – you are going to do the work.' All fourteen consultants voted yes and agreed to start immediately. I made an agreement with the union that my assignment was to coach the team in order to turn the company around from loss-making to at least breaking even at the end of the next financial year. We had eight months to change the course of the business dramatically.

47

Since consultants at Komanco were out of the office most days, spread across the country leading courses in different municipalities, they met face-to-face for only one day every six weeks. We agreed that in addition to this we would have a team conference call once a fortnight on Thursday evenings. The fact that I was supposed to be on maternity leave was quite useful in helping us stick to this arrangement. As luck would have it, my son was a very easy baby and slept a lot so when I had to go to the Komanco office every six weeks for the team meeting, my husband and baby would join me as well.

Our first team meeting was on a conference call on the 15th of March 2001. We discussed the lack of shared vision and highlighted some key questions. As I was handing the responsibility of the business over to the team, it was important to me that they had a map and a compass at least. Just as I had done at Freys Hotel, we also established on the call that the whole group was now 'the management team.' From here onwards, everyone was equally responsible – there would be no higher power, no managers, no subordinates. There was a board, of course, but it was the team and the team alone who were responsible for saving the company and my role was to coach them to success.

What's holding us back?

Before I joined, a department meeting had been booked for the beginning of April. The term 'department' had struck me as odd considering there were only fourteen employees at the time! This was in fact symptomatic of one of the issues holding the company back. Most of the consultants at Komanco had been recruited from the union, a huge organisation with over half a million members, which was incredibly siloed so many of them had little experience of working in an ordinary business. It was obvious from the beginning that there was a huge problem with sales. Historically, it had been the CEO's responsibility to manage the sales pipeline and the turnover of CEOs had been quite rapid. This meant that no one in the current team had any way of tracking sales so one of the first things the team agreed was to create a simple spreadsheet that could do this which would be open and accessible to everyone. This would be essential to generating profit. When it came to the question of who would take responsibility for updating this document, a woman called Harriet spoke up. 'I have no idea how to use Microsoft Excel,' she said, 'but I'm willing to learn. It's a bit scary for me but I've been wanting to learn for ages. So if it's ok with the group, I'll volunteer to take responsibility for this.' In the 1990s, it was a trend to aspire to be a 'learning organisation' but very few businesses actually achieved this because of a lack of communication between teams. However I've seen that when you decentralise power and distribute authority, it immediately triggers an intense phase of personal development and learning because teams and individuals are suddenly forced to upskill themselves. In this case, Harriet became extremely competent in Excel because it was her responsibility and it was so critical to the team's success.

Meanwhile, I had already noticed a lot of things going on in the group that weren't being discussed openly. There was a very palpable tense atmosphere. I brought this up and explained that we needed to work this out if we were going to create a strong sense of cooperation in the team. Although the team had been complicit in creating this culture of silence at Komanco, they understood from their theoretical training as leadership consultants that this wasn't healthy.

Pillar #2: A focus on working climate

Karin developed a process back in the nineties called Co-operation Coaching because she realised that building a group's capacity to develop a healthy, effective working climate was crucial for a group to be successful. This resonates with Will Schutz and his FIRO Theory as well as group development researchers like Susan Wheelan and Amy Edmondson who have found that high performing teams have, among other things, open communication structures and effective conflict management strategies. In a self-managing team, it's essential to be able to notice when the team climate is less than optimal and put it up on the table as a problem to solve together.

In most organisations, there is little to no focus on the working climate. Discussions about team performance tend to be limited to operational, 'surface' issues – strategy, process, procedure, tasks and so on. What most of us don't dare to talk about are the taboo issues, the things beneath the surface. Yet these are so often precisely the things that get in the way for teams to be effective. Conflict-avoidance in the workplace is endemic in most cultures around the world, and it destroys the working climate. Conflicts drain our energy as we tiptoe around them or get stuck in blaming and arguing. The reality is, there's enormous power and creativity on the other side of conflicts. If we could change our attitude towards conflict and learn to see the inherent value in them, we could improve our organisations and our results.

'Rather than wasting precious time and eroding personal relationships, conflict can be an opportunity for building new understanding, respect, and trust... Tensions are to be expected when teaming. Although rarely fun, tensions are not always bad. They can evoke creativity, sharpen ideas, and refine analyses. But there's a catch: patience, wisdom, and skill are needed to transform tensions into positive results. This is because most of us naturally resist tensions and the conflict they invariably bring.' Amy Edmondson, *Teaming*

SURFACE ISSUES

CLIMATE
(beneath the surface)
– Feelings, emotions
– Relationships
– Ways of being
– Mindset

Why do we tend to talk about surface issues instead of the things that really make a difference?

- Most of us have normalised our complaints about the working climate ('That's just the way things are around here')
- We think it'll be uncomfortable or awkward to confront things under the surface
- We have a collective belief (inherited from traditional command and control-style organisations) that talking about things like relationships, feelings, or ways of being isn't 'work'
- We're scared of hurting people's feelings
- We're scared of the consequences, we might be punished for speaking out or 'making things worse'
- We aren't aware that anything is going on under the surface
- We think we might be the only one who thinks something isn't right and we don't want to be disruptive or a 'buzzkill'

Moose heads

The Cooperation Coaching process Karin developed that we use today with clients is a facilitated dialogue to support the group to name the current climate and identify what they need in order to move forward and to create a desirable working climate. Part of this process involves talking about the 'moose heads' in the team. A moose head in this context is a metaphor for an issue that's become infected in the team (the Swedish equivalent of the elephant in the room). Usually, moose heads fall into three categories: (1) unresolved issues from the past,

(2) relationship dynamics, and (3) an individual or individuals' way of being. It's not the moose head (the details of what it is or the context) that's the problem, it's what has caused it to become infected and what's needed to let it go that we're interested in. All the while it's not being addressed, it's costing energy and effectiveness as people try to work around it. Imagine a bloody, rotting moose head on the table covered in flies. No one in the room dares talk about it, but it's there, taking up space and polluting the air. The process of bringing up moose heads can be very uncomfortable, but it's extremely effective for rapidly improving a team's working climate and cooperation, and it's so rewarding coming out the other side with trust, respect, and safety – the qualities we all long for in our workplaces.

Leading this process takes practice and skill and it's not something that can be taught in a book but rather something you need to experience and get plenty of feedback and coaching on. With that caveat, here are some of the key elements of the Cooperation Coaching process which starts to build the capacity in the team to talk about and work with climate.

Shifting a working climate

Step 1: Ask for the mandate

The first thing to do is to give the group the opportunity to choose to participate in this process. Without this, people are likely to remain in the parent-child dynamic, waiting for you to clean up their climate for them. To have the group be responsible for their climate, you need to say something about the purpose of the process (to develop a more productive, desirable working climate) and how it will be. Give people the chance to ask questions that will help them decide if they trust you and if they're willing to participate in the process. Similar to the concordance decision making process outlined in Chapter 1, listen to all questions and concerns and only move forward if there is a clear 'yes' from everyone involved.

Step 2: Describe the current working climate and identify the desired working climate

Ask the group to individually reflect on and describe the state of their current working climate. Remember, they're describing the atmosphere, what's underneath the surface. You can have them write down adjectives on Post-It notes and then have people group them into themes on the wall. If there are any Post-Its listing business or surface issues, distinguish that we are talking about climate and park them to one side.

Next, ask them to write down adjectives that describe the kind of working climate they would like. (Typically, people write things like 'open,' 'trusting,' 'productive,' and 'fun.') Stick these up on another space on the wall and again group them into themes. Now the group can quite literally see the gap between their current climate and their desired climate.

Step 3: Distinguish, clarify and listen

Returning to the current working climate, see if you can distinguish and clarify how it is currently. And then listen so that the group feels heard and 'felt.' The way to do this is by:

- Allowing things to be as they are – remember the 'Being able to be with it' cornerstone of the coaching mindset from Chapter 1. Your way of being is crucial – don't judge or convey that 'this should be some other way,' simply acknowledge how it is

- Mirror and state what you notice both above and below the surface
- Find themes, summarise
- Possibly go deeper – you might choose to fish for anything else that might be there to ensure everything is put up on the table

Step 4: Coach the group to become constructive

The main aim here is to place the responsibility of transforming any conflict or developing a desirable working climate with the group. Your job is to coach the group to become constructive. Usually, there are three areas you can support with:

- Carrying out moose heads – Distinguish the nature of any moose heads that come up by asking 'what is 'infected' in this issue? What is it that makes it uncomfortable?' To 'carry out' these moose heads, ask the individual or the group 'What is needed for you to put this behind you?' It could be things like an apology or being heard in something.
- Shifting an unproductive mindset to a productive mindset – You might hear a group is having an unproductive mindset in relation to creating a climate of cooperation. For example, for a group that's reluctant to take responsibility or blames external factors for the group's dysfunctions you might say something like: 'As long as you continue to see yourselves as victims and totally powerless, you won't be able to create the climate you want. It's only the people

in this room who can create something different. Can you consider the possibility or see the value in finding a more productive, helpful mindset?' (Note: it's crucial to have an adult-adult tone when distinguishing things in this way, otherwise it comes across as judgmental and critical)

- Finding strategies to break an unproductive dynamics – One way to do this is to create agreements or even code words. 'Would it be ok that X points out when you, Y, fall into your pitfall and become closed, and vice versa?'

You can then help the group draw up some key commitments to have them work towards and maintain the desired working climate. At this point, it's crucial that you don't add anything as a facilitator, however tempting. Usually, the group doesn't succeed 100% in sticking to their commitments regarding their working climate and needs to reconvene to either adjust what they agreed or strengthen their commitment to having it work. This learning is important in order for them to develop their own capacity to be responsible for their working climate. You can facilitate a follow-up session to review progress or carry out any further moose heads that have emerged or weren't addressed previously.

Once you've initiated the process of starting to talk about climate, you can encourage anyone to bring up the climate whenever they notice something going on. Of course you can do this as a leader or facilitator, but even better to have everyone in the group responsible for doing this when they feel the need. Here's a simple overview of the process:

1. When discussing 'surface issues,' listen under the surface as well and distinguish any climate going on separate from the issues. If you think you hear something...
2. Name the climate and put it up on the table. Do this clearly, candidly, and succinctly until people 'get it.'
3. Listen to whatever comes up afterwards so the group feels heard, allow everything to be as it is, mirror, summarise, and surface anything else that wants to be said.
4. Coach the group to become constructive by stating again how it is, distinguishing any moose heads, unproductive mindsets or dynamics, and then support the group to choose how they want to move forward with them, whether it's carrying out a moose head, choosing a new mindset, or creating agreements.

Moose heads on the table

At Komanco, the first moose head the team brought up was an unresolved issue from the past. They called the moose head 'mysterious disappearances,' in reference to a string of colleagues who had gone missing without explanation. Some people joked it was as if there were trapdoors in the floor. The group convinced me this was how it felt. In reality, former CEOs had made decisions about individuals who needed to leave the business without communicating anything to the team because they seldom met face-to-face. So consultants would turn up to a meeting and there would be an empty chair but no one would say anything. People just assumed the person must have quit and moved on. But amongst themselves, the fourteen consultants began to talk about this 'mysterious disappearances' phenomenon. I asked them what they needed to resolve this issue and they agreed they wanted to ask some questions of those responsible, giving them an opportunity to explain the rationale behind the decisions. Lars-Åke and some of the other CEOs were able to dispel the sense of mystery but more importantly, the team were finally able to talk about it out in the open. The group was united in agreeing they wouldn't let this happen again because everyone would be involved in the decisions from now on.

The next moose head was harder to shift. It concerned a myth that the team had created about three of its members. These three appeared to have an informal subgroup which met in secret to steer the business without involving the others. This had been going on for years and even had a name: The Secret Troika. The three accused were totally shocked and insisted it wasn't true. However, the mistrust in the group was deeply ingrained and we discussed it for a long time. In the end, the team agreed to trust that there was no secret troika from now on.

Having discussed their moose heads for several hours, the group expressed that they felt the ceiling was much higher and they felt able to speak much more openly now. We went on to deal with business issues. One old complaint was about the administration system they'd inherited from the union which was fine for an organisation for 600,000 members, but costly and cumbersome for Komanco with its small team of fourteen. The accounts were also run by the union's finance department which we later discovered was a huge problem. So the team decided that Eva and Åsa would quickly generate some suggestions for improving the administration system. Now the group had the authority to decide what they wanted to change immediately, no one was able to play the role of the victim.

The months went by and after we returned from the summer holidays, the secret troika myth reared its ugly head once more. We had a conference call to address the mistrust this moose head was generating. For me it was clear that everyone was working towards the same outcome, but individuals misinterpreted each other's actions, believing people had hidden agendas and bad intentions. It was really painful to see how this was hindering their cooperation so I used this opportunity to raise it. Sometimes, a coach can channel the frustration he or she experiences and use it to empower a person or a group, so long as you are super aware that your tone is not one of an annoyed parent or boss. It can help create a sense of urgency, raising the stakes to the level of 'this is your life.' So I did this by stating very clearly, and with a little more frankness than usual, that the team was not behaving in a trustful way and a gossip culture was getting in the way of their ability to work together. And then I was silent. No one spoke on the call for a long, long time. Finally, one person spoke up. 'You're right,' they said. 'We need to stop distrusting each other. My suggestion is we start right now.' And in that moment, something shifted for good.

A crisis meeting

After patiently waiting for the financial reports from the union's finance department, on the 3rd of October we finally received some figures. We were informed that the income was on track, but the costs were 1 million SEK (100,000 Euros) too high. I couldn't understand it, how could our costs be too high when we had been on track in August? The next day, we received a totally different report which said the costs were on track but we were 2.5 million SEK behind our sales target. Our conference call booked for the 4th of October became a crisis meeting. The finances were a nightmare and everyone was scared. This wakeup call, however, also provided us with a valuable insight. The team at last understood what was wrong with the company. They realised that what they had been counting as sales were actually just informal agreements with municipalities. For many of these 'done deals' there were no purchase orders or training delivery dates set. Consultants had been celebrating these agreements with clients and in their haste, hadn't followed up with them to book the dates. The obvious solution was to start an intense phase of booking in dates on these offers before Christmas to get the figures to where they needed to be. There was a mutual understanding that it was everyone's role to generate sales and win new customers, but two consultants were particularly skilled at this.

What then became very clear, and had previously never been discussed in the open, was that the remaining consultants were really worried about living up to the standards set by these two sales stars. They were too paralysed with fear to even pick up the phone. We put this issue up on the table and everyone agreed that depending on two people for sales wasn't sufficient to create a profitable business and sustain fourteen consultants. They decided to split themselves into two teams, one for the north of the country and one for the south, with one of the two strong salespeople in each. The team agreed to view sales as a group responsibility – each person might contribute in different ways, but the key was to cooperate as opposed to each individual running their own race. Komanco had a long list of customers and great contacts so the team was able to replace the mindset that 'sales = cold calls' with 'talking to people I have a relationship with,' which was a big relief to many of them. The team agreed on goals and scheduled frequent calls to update each other.

The lure of the heroic leader to the rescue

Before we received these disastrous financial reports, I had already booked a week-long trip to the United States and in those days, phoning Sweden from abroad for a conference call wasn't straightforward. When the crisis hit, I seriously considered cancelling my flight. But I reminded myself of two things. First, my presence wouldn't make a difference anyway since I wasn't operationally involved and knew very little about the products so I would have been no help on the phone to customers. And second, I recognised that I was experiencing the primal instinct many managers have. When times are good, it's much easier for us to be coaching and empowering and get out of the way. But when a crisis happens, suddenly we dare not trust anyone but ourselves and we rush in to fix the situation. However, to charge in like a knight on horseback completely undermines all of a team's newfound power and authority. I realised that my absence was an opportunity to underline that the team at Komanco was truly on its own and the responsibility to save the day was theirs and theirs alone. Of course, that didn't stop me from worrying! It would be one of the toughest weeks of my career, testing my faith in such a hands-off approach.

I came back from the US in time for our fortnightly team conference call, anxious to hear the team's results. It was now the middle of October. I needn't have been nervous because the miraculous had happened: both teams had achieved fantastic results. Team South had hit their target, and Team North had exceeded their by a factor of three! It was a huge accomplishment. Our new focus became about not losing grip and continuing the good work.

A huge accomplishment

After our sales turning point, we had an intense autumn at Komanco with lots of training being delivered across the country. We finished the season with a team Christmas dinner. At this point, we speculated that we might even generate a profit of a couple of hundred thousand SEK, which would have been totally unimaginable at the start of the year. When we got the year-end figures in February, the accounts showed that Komanco had actually turned over 3.3 million SEK in profit! Both the team and the board questioned the accuracy of the results because they were so unbelievable and we'd had issues with the reports from the union's finance team in the past. But a large auditing firm confirmed it: the 3.3 million SEK in profit was there. We also learned that the turnover had increased by 2 million Swedish Krona to 14 million SEK. Remember, the year before there had been a loss of 4.4 million SEK! So the company was profitable, the team was now in charge and I was able to move on. Looking back, it's clear the team made this transformation possible. When I added it all up, during the eight months as CEO of Komanco I had worked a total of just eighteen days.

The team decided they wanted to select a new CEO from within the group rather than appoint one externally. They were really keen on keeping this way of working and that the CEO would just be a coordinator and a like to the board, rather than a manager. So one of the last things I did as CEO was facilitate the group to make their decision. IT was a thorough concordance process of more than three hours. I remember at one point being a little too hasty in interpreting that the group had made a choice. They insisted they weren't there yet and we resumed the discussion. It proved to me that the group had become very skilled in thorough decision making and has also taken the responsibility to challenge me as a facilitator. In the end, everyone was very happy to stand behind Åsa Kullberg as the new CEO and she would remain in that position for several years to come. The team also put together instructions for the CEO that would guarantee this new way of working stayed in place.

Extract from instructions to the new CEO

1. Documentation of current ways of operating (January 2002)

The founding principle in March 2001 was to integrate the 'Bottom-up approach' in Komanco with Karin Tenelius as the CEO. All employees were aligned and had a say in choosing this road with Karin as the coach (and CEO). Consequently, ways of working have taken form and evolved, as described below. All employees at Komanco will be named 'the management team,' which is the title we have used since April 2001.

Responsibility

The management team is accountable for Komanco's business being run successfully, which means:

- In line with Komanco's values
- In line with the Komanco vision and mission
- Reaching a level of profitability agreed upon by the owners (the board)
- The employees of Komanco 'own' the business 'mentally' (but not legally) *i.e.* they see themselves as accountable for running Komanco successfully. (This is how it is today in January 2002, which shows in the results.)

From March to December of 2001, the CEO's role has been to coach and empower the management team to reconstruct the company in line with their plans, in order to reach their goals and become profitable. The management team has made their decisions without the CEO, who has, regardless, been present at all meetings.

For the future CEO, the instructions below have been created by the management team.

The CEO's accountabilities

Regarding the board:

The CEO is accountable regarding the board to make sure the business follows the strategic decisions made by the board, and to see that the business is run successfully and is profitable. The CEO is the management team's representative when meeting with the board.

Regarding the management team:
- Make sure the team has access to up-to-date financial information (the CEO doesn't need to do this, but rather needs to see that it happens)
- Make sure the financial information has been processed with the frequency decided by the management team
- Make sure there are concrete formulations made regarding goals, action points, and who's accountable
- Make sure the agreed ways of operating are complied with

The CEO is responsible for major strategic issues being prepared and worked through in the management team and for presenting them to the board. The board will then decide and the CEO will report the board's decision back to the management team.

These major strategic issues are:
- Business vision and mission
- Values
- Strategic crossroads about what markets to act on
- Other crossroads
- Investments exceeding SEK 200,000

Operational matters (actions and plans) are decided in the management team.

We also rewrote the instructions to the board to have them aligned with this new way of working at Komanco. All initiatives and suggestions would come from the new management team (i.e. all employees) and the board's task was to accept them, rather than trying to steer the company. What was really fascinating was also that the board's view of the employees had shifted from 'they are incompetent' to 'they are skilled and trustworthy' in just eight months.

In 2002, the team at Komanco started to work without me and by spring, they had more great financial results. In spite of their success, they realised they had too many consultants to support on the income they were generating. It was clear the owner wouldn't accept another year of losses so the team would need to downsize to guarantee profitability. It would be their biggest challenge yet, but now they had a healthy working climate and the dialogue skills to handle it. The team realised they needed to lose three consultants and were able to come to a decision using concordance with dignity and respect. Komanco remained profitable every year until the owner eventually decided to sell the company in 2009 in order to focus on their core activities as a union.

Summary

- Coaching the team at Komanco confirmed for me that a focus on working climate and carrying out moose heads in the team is crucial to a self-managing team's performance.
- No matter how big the crisis or how tempting the call of the heroic leader, it's only when you truly trust people and get out of the way that a group can achieve the seemingly impossible.
- The work with Komanco was important to me because I now had tangible business results for a self-managing way of working for those who were primarily interested in the bottom line.

3. A string of failures: lessons about business owners

'Conversations about empowerment always seem to turn to a discussion of how we are going to change other people.'

Peter Block, *Stewardship*

I now had two strong self-management case studies: a hotel already performing well achieving even better results, and a training company that went from loss to profit in under a year. But I would learn some difficult lessons over the next few years about what it takes for self-management to be successful and, more importantly, for it to stick.

In the early 2000s, I supported a number of companies to transition to self-management including three in the restaurant industry, which is, in my experience, an industry with some of the most challenging, ingrained hierarchical climates. All of these businesses benefited hugely from the Cooperation Coaching climate shifting process. However, with all three of the restaurant companies I ran into problems with the owners. What I came to realise is that there are two reasons why a self-managing way of organising fails to stick when it comes to owners:

- It's not what the owner signed up for
- The owner doesn't have the skill or will to be a coaching, empowering leader (which is, as we explored in the Freys Hotel story, the first pillar of an effective self-managing team)

It's not what the owner signed up for

Despite my years of experience, I've always found it incredibly difficult to truly convey what it takes to be a top leader in a self-managing organisation. I tell people it's extremely challenging and it essentially means making yourself redundant. They nod and smile and say, 'That's great! I'd love to be more hands off and have more time!' Yet even when they see the great results self-management can deliver in their teams, several owners I've worked with grow to miss the feeling of being needed and being the person who saves and fixes things. When the team starts to take responsibility and operations can run without the owner, they often complain to me that this wasn't what they signed up for and revert back to their old, top-down ways.

The owner doesn't have the skill or will to be a coaching, empowering leader

The reality is, not everyone has the capacity to be a coaching, empowering leader. I've met many leaders who think they can be empowering (and in the past I've made the mistake of believing them) but very quickly I've seen the real impact they have on their team. If you cannot give power and authority away, your team will never really trust that they are responsible and you'll never see the full benefits or potential of self-management. Many managers have got to where they are because they have a lot of drive, enthusiasm and energy, or perhaps because they're smart and great at problem-solving. It's hard for them to accept that these very qualities are now what will prevent them from unleashing their team's potential if they lack self-awareness. You might even say that managers and entrepreneurs are often the least-equipped to become coaching, empowering leaders.

I've also found that many leaders simply don't have the will to develop their abilities in terms of leadership. Once they realise that having a self-managing team means they need to train their own abilities such as listening and coaching, their motivation and interest often wanes. Again, it doesn't matter if I state this up front. Perhaps they overestimate their current abilities or underestimate the journey of becoming a coaching leader. It's challenging and involves painful insights, confronting blind spots and pitfalls, getting lots of tough feedback – something that requires real commitment. For a manager who is perhaps used to being the hero, there's no reward in the team doing it for themselves because they don't experience this as having anything to do with a person's leadership.

Summary

- What I learned from this string of failures was how crucial the mindset of the owner or CEO is in terms of whether an organisation can be successfully self-managing or not.
- Embarking on this transformation journey means a seismic shift in the role of the owner or CEO – many

leaders enjoy being needed and operationally involved and aren't willing to give this up.

- This process also requires an enormous commitment to self-development for all leaders, especially those formerly at 'the top'. Nothing will change if leaders believe that change only happens 'out there.'

4. Excosoft: a spiral of profit and loss

'A company's job isn't to empower people; it's to remind people that they walk in the door with power and to create the
conditions for them to exercise it.'

Patty McCord, *Power*

This is the story of a company I coached as an interim CEO
and is a good example of who it's possible to get great results
within a short space of time with self-management but also
how quickly this way of working can be undone when a new
CEO takes over if they aren't a coaching, empowering leader.

In September 2005, a meeting was booked to liquidate an
IT company after years of financial struggles. My husband's
brother, Jan Christian, had founded the business in 1986. It
was his life, his dream, his passion. Now he found himself in a
room with a liquidation lawyer instructed to 'kill it'. At the last
minute, Jan Christian and our business partner Fredi managed
to convince the investors to sell their shares to us, making us the
majority shareholders. The plan was for me to step in as CEO
and use my self-management approach to turn the business
around. I knew absolutely nothing about IT, of course, but I saw
this as an advantage – it would make it much easier for the employees to find their own solutions for getting the company back on its
feet as opposed to relying on a charismatic leader to save them.

71

I quickly discovered that the employees at Excosoft were not only incredibly competent in their technical field but they were also extremely talented project leaders and salespeople. Even though they knew I would be bringing no technical knowledge, it was hard for them to shake the expectation that I would somehow solve all their problems, perhaps because they had been used to a succession of CEOs who had seduced them with heroic visions to rescue the company. I had a handover meeting with the latest CEO who spent over three hours taking me through all the tasks and responsibilities he had. At the time, the headcount had gone from around fifty people to just ten. I remember actually thinking at the end of our meeting, 'hmmm, so nothing, really!' because all of it was checking and controlling, and I wouldn't be doing any of that.

From doom to possibility

We began our work in November and I started by distinguishing the climate at Excosoft. The atmosphere was very tense. People were understandably scared and disheartened after years of adversity and the recent threat of liquidation. Until recently, Monday morning management meetings frequently featured the CEO chanting: 'We have to sell more! We have to sell more!' I've learned that when I'm coaching teams like this, the first thing that's important is to listen to people so they feel heard. One reason is to get a sense of the nature of the current climate, but listening is also extremely valuable because it starts to build a culture of psychological safety – a term Amy Edmondson defines in her book *The Fearless Organisation* as 'as a climate in which people are comfortable expressing and being themselves'. Of course, being a great listener (and indeed coach) doesn't mean you have to agree with everything someone says or pander to them like a caring parent. So often all people need is to feel heard and suddenly, they're able to reclaim their power.

Insight #2: The gold in listening

'Listening is at the source of all great leadership. It is a core skill, not only for leadership, but for all domains of professional mastery.'

Otto Scharmer, Presencing Institute

Practicing your ability to listen is the most important task for a coaching leader, and a crucial part of being an effective team member in a self-managing organisation. It's difficult to distinguish listening as an ability, and listening as just a function of hearing what someone is saying. When we talk about listening, we mean listening not just to what is being said, but to what is not being said, to who the person is, and listening for what's missing, for what needs to be accomplished. In other words, listening is about more subtle, elusive things than just spoken words. Without being able to listen, you can't ask the kind of coaching questions that move things forward. The clues for what questions to ask are in what you hear, not in your own head. We believe if people really knew the true value of listening and how many unexpected results lie on the other side of it – efficiency, life-changing moments, money, decisions, ownership – there would be a listening gym on every corner and people would flock to spend hours training their listening skills.

There are two outcomes of this kind of listening. The first is that when you truly listen, rather than interpret, it can reveal invaluable insights and empower people. For example, you can listen for what's in the way for someone to achieve their goal, or listen for what's really important to them, or listen for what's missing in order for a group to make a decision. The second outcome of listening in this way is that a person feels heard and 'felt,' having an experience of being truly 'gotten' by another human being. This takes care of the receptors in the reptilian and emotional part of our brains, freeing up capacity for us to think clearly and creatively and take action. Truly listening to someone can clear the fog for them to see a way forward and draw on their own potential.

Ultimately, what you are aiming for is a way of *being* that *is* listening. The way to access this way of being is to practice some behavioural things that might feel a bit awkward and inauthentic at first, but over time can become integrated into your own way of doing things.

The starting point is to become a beginner again and realise just how little we actually listen to each other as human beings. Invite colleagues, friends and loved ones to give you feedback on how you listen to them. Build in moments of reflection after meetings or conversations to evaluate your own listening – was I listening so that person felt truly heard and felt? Or was I just listening until it was my turn to talk? Or listening to analyse what they're saying so I can offer a solution? Or listening so I can appear to be good at listening?

Here are some access points into developing a listening way of being:

• Summarise and confirm what you've heard: 'So what I'm hearing you say is [their words]... is that right?'

• Mirror feelings: 'I can hear that you're feeling really frustrated...'

• If you find it hard to listen in certain situations, you can use the MAP Skill from Alan Watkin's book *4D Leadership* when you notice yourself being triggered:

- Move your attention away from your own thinking and drop into the body and breathe;
- Appreciate the speaker (appreciate here means listening with unconditional positive regard – you don't have to agree with what they're saying, but you can consider that this is their view and it's valid);
- Play back the underlying meaning.

> • And finally, slow down! Many of us are always 'on our way' and in a hurry to move onto some kind of action. If you have a tendency to give people advice or offer solutions or be impatient, remind yourself that *this is not a problem to be solved, it is a human being to listen to.*

One day at Excosoft I listened to a man sharing his concerns for hours. He told me how doomed he felt the company was. He didn't dare contact any customers because he was a reliable person and so it would be risky and dishonest. I listened to him so he felt heard but left all the responsibility with him. Just by being able to voice his fears, he was able to consider that the company might be saveable. He suddenly became very productive and landed a huge client. It wasn't a new lead, he'd known it was a ripe opportunity for a while but hadn't felt able to contact them until now. This sale resulted in the company becoming profitable again just five weeks after I became CEO, giving us the breathing space we needed, and giving others the energy and confidence to close more deals. We were stable again.

Two climate issues

In terms of the climate, two main issues surfaced that were getting in the way of the team being effective. The first issue that became apparent was that people at Excosoft had been discussing what was best for the company for ten years but it had always been all talk and no action. I decided my role was to help them distinguish the essence of these strategies, dusting them off and enabling the team to get a shared picture of them.

One pitfall we often have as leaders is to come with our own opinions or new strategies instead of trusting that the people who have worked there for years are competent and know what is or isn't working.

The other big challenge at Excosoft was the resignation that hung in the air. People felt that they weren't able to do what they knew they really should and the faith in the capacity to make things happen as a team was really low. People needed to believe that even though something hadn't been done before, it was still possible.

Pillar #3: A culture of mandate and involvement

The final pillar we believe is crucial for becoming an effective self-managing team or organisation is creating a culture of mandate and involvement. True engagement and responsibility comes from an ability to influence or have a say in our work and circumstances. Choice is perhaps *the* defining feature of an adult-adult paradigm of working together. Something shifts when we are given both the responsibility for something and the mandate or authority to decide what to do about it. When people feel truly involved and accountable, all sorts of ideas, solutions, systems, and structures are created in service of the team and the level of commitment to making them happen is next-level.

Mandate might seem like a strange word in the context of self-management because we often associate it with being ordered to do something. However, mandate is a powerful tool in a self-managing organisation. For our purposes, let's distinguish mandate as *the given permission or the authority to do something*. Particularly if you're a leader, there are two useful habits you can develop regarding mandate. The first is to get the mandate, and the second is to give the mandate away.

Getting the mandate

Let's go back to the Cooperation Coaching process we outlined in Chapter 2 as an example and look at the 'getting the mandate' part in more detail. Often we are brought in by a manager or the HR team of an organisation to facilitate Cooperation Coaching with a team, which almost always means the team hasn't had a say in choosing us or this process. If we really want teams to become responsible for their own working climate, they need to have the opportunity to *choose* this process. Without this opportunity to choose, the best-case scenario is people will be well-behaved or even engaged participants but they won't really feel ownership for the process and therefore the results will be limited. (The worst-case scenario is they will either be quietly sceptical, or reluctant to the point of sabotaging the process.) So, here's what we do at the start of any Cooperation Coaching process:

- **Clearly state the purpose of the activity** – say something about the purpose and the potential value connected to the group's self-interest (we've never encountered a team that wasn't interested in having a more open, trusting and productive working climate).

- **Distinguish how it will be and what they're 'signing up to'** – say something briefly about what the process will look like and how it will be, how it will *feel*. Here it's also important to outline that *they* will do the work, you will be facilitating but they will produce the outcomes. This is almost like a mini contract for their involvement and responsibility. You can also say something about your role as facilitator and why they can trust you to lead this process.
- **Give the group the opportunity to ask clarifying questions** – ask: 'Are there any questions you have that would help you to choose to take part in this process? Or that would help you put your trust in me to facilitate it?' Remember that the purpose of your answers is to clarify so they can make an informed decision, not to convince them. People can smell the difference a mile away!
- **Give them the opportunity to choose** – tell the group they can now choose whether or not they want to go ahead with the process. Be very clear that they have the opportunity to say no!

Sometimes getting the mandate takes minutes, other times it can take several hours. It might seem pedantic but it's incredibly important because without getting the group's mandate, you as the facilitator have the lion's share (if not all) of the responsibility for the process and therefore the dynamic is parent-child again. You can feel a shift in the energy in the room when a group votes 'yes' – now they are jointly responsible and truly active participants in co-creating an outcome.

If you are a leader, you can use these steps for getting the mandate any time you want to initiate something in the team or organisation for which you want people to be involved in and responsible for. It's a good way to unlearn the habit of using your inherited authority to push projects or suggestions onto people, or assuming you have people's involvement and commitment already. If you're a team member or 'equal,' you can use this framework to get the mandate or authority needed to facilitate or lead something from your peers.

Giving away the mandate

Giving away the mandate and the authority is about constantly placing the problem with the individual or team. If you're a leader (or used to be a manager), you'll find that individuals and groups are usually very skilled at (unconsciously) giving you back the problem. However tempting it is to take it, don't accept it. It is in the team that the responsibility should lie, it is here that solutions should appear. Giving away the mandate involves three main activities as a coaching leader:

- Placing the responsibility (or problem) with the team and supporting it to be effective
- Creating opportunities for free, informed, and active choices which lead to team members assuming responsibility and ownership
- Listening so the team feels heard and then asking tough, coaching questions, giving feedback, and distinguishing what's getting in the way (*e.g.* naming an unproductive climate) – and then giving *that* problem to the team

Some examples of tough, coaching questions that work with individuals and groups are:

- What do you want to achieve in this conversation (goal, outcome)?
- How would you like it to be?
- What alternatives can you see?
- What do you need in order to [their words]...?
- What is missing for you to [their words]...?
- What is essential in order to [their words]...?
- What stops you from [their words]...?
- What could be the next (or first) step?
- How could you do [their words]?
- How can you move this forward?
- Say something more about that...

Again, the habit of giving away the mandate isn't exclusive to leaders. Being an effective team member means any time you spot victimhood, helplessness or blaming in the team, you can place the problem on the table and support the group to take responsibility for doing something about it.

In order to shift the climate of resignation at Excosoft, I did a lot of listening and asking tough, coaching questions that placed the problem with the team, like those listed in the Pillar #3 box. As always, it was important for me to have a coaching way of being when asking these questions. It would have the opposite effect if my tone sounded at all judgmental, impatient, or doubting. Instead, I related to the team's potential and trusted that they had all the resources they needed to solve their own problems. In Excosoft's case, the fact that I had no expertise in the IT sector made it easier to resist the temptation to give answers or solutions, and meant that the team really believed that only they could take responsibility for implementing these strategies. People finally started to whir into action.

By December, Excosoft was back in the black and a huge order arrived in January that put the company firmly back on its feet. Meetings and conversations became about how to be more effective and making decisions about getting work done. In February 2006, however, I began to notice tensions brewing between the founder, Jan Christian, and some of the other team members. I proposed a session to carry out the moose heads and we scheduled a half-day meeting to tackle them. We drew up a timeline of Excosoft's whole history and circled some of the infected issues that had emerged over time. One by one, we were able to clear up any misunderstandings. Two colleagues were able to share some candid feedback about a way of being Jan Christian had, a sort of 'cloud of stubborness' which often meant people felt they had to be careful around him. I facilitated the group to listen to each other, and the two felt satisfied when they understood Jan Christian didn't have any bad intentions. I asked them if they were willing to give him a second chance and they said yes. We ended the session with co-created agreements to take up any disagreements or incidents with each other immediately in future. To help, we identified a code phrase that anyone could invoke if Jan Christian was in one of his pitfalls in order to alert him to it and help him shift to a more open, trusting way of being. It was 'nobody's home,' referring to Jan Christian's tendency to be stone faced which caused people to wonder: 'Does he get what I'm saying? What is he thinking or feeling?!' I wrote in my diary entry for that day: 'Jan Christian made this process as effective as it was thanks to him having an angel's patience with the difficult environment. Hero!'

In 2006, the company had a profit of just over 3 million SEK and by the end of the year, had nearly doubled the number of employees. At this point, one of the new owners told me I was no longer needed. 'From here onwards,' he said, 'it's just going to be about strategy and technical stuff, which will be no fun for you.' I was happy I was no longer needed and agreed to leave. Here's how the founder Jan Christian reflected on the shift that happened in Excosoft years later when Lisa and I interviewed him:

> I'm a programmer, a nerd, and I founded this company in 1986 so I've been a CEO and a programmer over the years. I can't see the difference between a manager or a programmer or a receptionist – everyone contributes so for me, working in a flat way seems totally natural. So when people tried to impose some kind of a top-down structure in the company, it didn't feel good. Unfortunately I didn't listen to my gut feeling so I had all these strange things come into the company – venture capital, boards, and leaders who thought they understood but didn't. We're a small software company and we're making decisions every day as a team so it's difficult for a board to function in such an organisation. They feel they don't know what's happening because things move so quickly but they try to interfere. After a few years of the top-down structure, people became very bitter and there was a depressing atmosphere. People came in each morning and didn't say hello – it was a very sad place to work. And then we bought the company back from the venture capitalists and Karin came in and the energy changed. The fun thing was that we started to talk about things that were in the air and when we started to talk about things, it made it much more interesting.

From self-managing to controlling, and back again

Unfortunately, after I left, someone else took over as CEO. He was very enthusiastic at first but he quickly started to control things. Soon, there was frustration everywhere. Jan Christian remembers: 'He started to have meetings with the management team, so we had meetings every Monday morning and then we started having meetings before that to prepare what we should say. And there were only twelve people! It was just stupid.' After several years of this getting worse and worse, the decision was made for the CEO to leave Excosoft. It was painful for me to see the work we'd done to create a culture of involvement and responsibility at Excosoft be unravelled so quickly by a controlling style of leadership. Of course, the CEO who took over from me had all the best intentions and I thought he had the capacity to be an empowering leader, but clearly this wasn't the case.

Since the exit of that CEO, Excosoft has settled into something in between top-down and totally self-managing, a much leaner team with a fairly flat structure with Jan Christian as the CEO. 'Everything is really open now,' Jan Christian told us. 'Everyone trusts me, they know I don't have any hidden agenda. But some of the responsibilities have disappeared because it was so flat and we created groups for making decisions but somehow, some things didn't get done. My colleague is now helping create processes without being top-down. I think we will continue to be flat. Everyone likes it. When I ask people, they say they 'yes, we still want to be flat but we need some more processes and to be more organised.' So they miss that but they don't want managers back – absolutely not.'

Summary

- My work with Excosoft taught me that knowing nothing about the business sector can be really helpful when trying to resist the urge to offer advice or solutions and instead place the responsibility with the team or organisation.
- When people are listened to so that they feel heard, it can be a powerful catalyst in releasing their potential and propelling them into action.
- I experienced, again, that a coaching, empowering leader is essential to holding the space for self-management and preventing the organisation from slipping back into a top-down hierarchy.
- Not many people have the level of empowering skills needed to maintain self-management and I learned the hard way how important it is for me to manage my expectations of managers taking over after a transformation process. In my experience, it's best to avoid managers altogether!

So, across the three transformation stories (Freys Hotel, Komanco and Excosoft), we've outlined what we believe are the three pillars of developing an effective, self-managing organisation:
- **A coaching mindset and way of being**
- **A focus on working climate**
- **A culture of mandate and involvement**

Part 2
Two case studies of buying companies and giving the authority away

I had learned a lot from my phase of transforming companies as a consultant or interim CEO, but it had left me frustrated. To watch teams flourish in a climate of new-found authority and collaboration, and then see the weeds of command and control creep back in and strangle it was painful. It seemed like very few leaders were capable of holding the space for this way of working. And then one day in December 2008 I had a startling insight whilst sitting in the audience at a conference: I should buy the companies! As the owner I would have full authority to give all of the power away. This marked the beginning of a challenging phase in my career of buying and transforming businesses.

In this part of the book, I want to share the stories of two companies my business partners and I bought and transformed: a bankrupt healthcare company and a telemarketing company stuck in the dark ages. I learned a lot of harsh lessons during this period about the kinds of companies and conditions that make this transformation process almost impossible. In hindsight I can see that we were very naive in our purchasing decisions. Sometimes I console myself about the fact that I never went to the famous Swedish business school by considering the fact that the risks I took and money I lost is equivalent to the student loans I would have accrued as a graduate. The hands-on training I got from the following eight years of owning and transforming companies was extremely valuable.

With the healthcare company, we ran into all sorts of difficulties, such as a change in legislation, which made it very difficult for small companies in the healthcare industry to get financing. Ultimately, we ended up selling the business in 2014. With the call centre, we also had to deal with a lot of trying circumstances and in 2017, we made the tough decision together to close the business down.

The reason I want to share these stories is because the legacy of both of these endeavours is a human one. I witnessed employees at both the healthcare company and the call centre develop enormously and with their newfound self-esteem, many have gone onto new and exciting careers that wouldn't have been possible before. I also want to reflect on what I've learned in terms of the conditions I now believe are crucial for a self-managing organisation to be able to endure real hardships.

5. Elisabethgården: everyone a business owner

'Vulnerability doesn't come after trust – it precedes it. Leaping into the unknown, when done alongside others, causes the solid ground of trust to materialise beneath our feet.'

Daniel Coyle, *The Culture Code*

Excited by my new idea but lacking the funds, I proposed to my Tuff Leadership Training colleagues that we should pool our money in order to buy and transform companies. We discussed it at length, airing our concerns and hesitations, and eventually decided to go ahead. In 2009 we bought our first company, a healthcare company called Elisabethgården that had gone bankrupt in a region of central Sweden. Elisabethgården served municipalities around Sweden by temporarily housing families in need and coaching them on how to function again. We purchased the building and re-employed around five people that had been laid off. We also changed the business idea from coaching the families to producing reports on the parents' skills to take care of the children. These reports take eight weeks to complete while they're living in the facility and the report is then used by the social authorities to decide whether the children should stay with the parents. We also offered shelter for threatened mothers and children.

Building a climate of openness

I started to coach the employees every third week or so and one of the biggest challenges was the working climate. Elisabeth-gården had experienced many different kinds of owners, from dedicated visionaries in the beginning to 'spreadsheet owners' who were more interested in numbers than people. This meant it took a long time for employees to truly trust us as the new owners and it was hard for people to be honest and straightforward with each other. Swedish shyness and low self-esteem were prevalent. Everyone agreed they wanted to create an open climate based on acceptance and trust, but the eternal complaint was that they didn't know how. In my experience, this is less of an excuse and more an indication that the working climate isn't yet safe enough for people to take risks and be vulnerable. But to create a safe climate requires openness which means you have to train people and support them in being open even before it feels safe, encouraging them to be brave. I've learned that it helps to single out a few individuals that are a bit braver and ask the group to give them the mandate to lead the way until eventually the culture starts to shift. After that it becomes easier to maintain because there is support from a larger number of people.

The work of shifting the climate to a reliable, sustainable quality of open, straightforward communication is sometimes challenging and discouraging. It can be easy to give up. However, my belief that this is utterly crucial for effective self-managing teams drives me to persevere even when it seems stuck. At Elisabethgården it became a mix of push and pull. I would push and challenge the group to be more open, then I would be silent and calm and see if the climate surfaced in the group. I created an open dialogue with the team by asking them coaching questions like: Given that you want a more open climate, what do you need? How are you stuck? What does this fear look like? What's maintaining the grip of the status quo? Everyone desperately wanted a more open climate, but really struggled to make it happen. People often shared they didn't know how to do it. These were individuals with many years of studying communication and psychology and experience in having supportive client conversations, so they knew all about this subject in theory. But the habit of speaking openly and resolving issues together as a team was new territory. What it took was persistence – bringing the subject up again and again and confronting together the lack of straightforward communication. I learned that this process demands an unwavering commitment and a lot of patience.

New-found autonomy

One thing that happened very early on was people embracing their new-found autonomy. The handyman, for example, turned out to be a purchasing wizard. When I talked to him, I could tell he had a talent for remembering figures and finding bargains. The business began to grow and there was a need for more technical equipment like TVs, a more industrial lawn mower, additional cars for the business and so on. It was clear he would know how to get the best deal and so the team gave him the mandate to do all the negotiating with the suppliers. Whether it was a new freezer or painting the buildings, he would get the best deal and create mutually beneficial payment terms. Since no one else had this interest, he became a valuable source and grew as a person with this appreciated expertise of his.

I also remember the first time an employee told me on the phone: 'By the way, we bought another car. We thought of asking you for permission but then decided against it.' I was overjoyed! This might not sound that extraordinary, but keep in mind these were people who had been employed as caregivers and had never been involved in the finances of the organisation before. Here was a large investment and they had considered it carefully and made the decision by themselves.

Insight #3: Transparency and self-set salaries

When it comes to transparency, Jan Carlzon, the former CEO of Scandinavian Airline Systems (SAS) who transformed the organisation by empowering employees to deliver exceptional service, says it all:

'An individual without information can't take responsibility.
An individual with information can't help but take responsibility.'

It's crucial to open up all company information to employees, otherwise they can't take responsibility for the business. However, making it available isn't enough – it has to be meaningful and understandable, otherwise people won't know what to do with it.

Spanish consultancy K2K Emocionando has successfully transformed more than 50 organisations in the Basque country over the last fifteen years. One of the principles they've developed in their transformation process is to immediately open up all information and create accessible financial reports for employees. They help set up quarterly meetings to inform people and train them on how to understand the company's finances.

Once company finances are totally transparent, many teams decide they want to review salaries and design a new process together. However, exploring self-managed, open salaries is no easy feat and we wouldn't recommend starting with this if your team or organisation is new to self-organising. Money is often a contentious subject because we project all sorts of values, assumptions and insecurities onto it. What's more, when you open up salaries it can unleash feelings of anger and unfairness when employees see the differences they weren't previously aware of.

One question we get asked a lot is: 'How can we make sure salaries are fair?' There are many different models for self-managed salaries and you'll have to discover and design the one that's right for your organisation. But let's briefly explore the word 'fair.' My friend and fellow consultant Tom Nixon has learned from experience that fair is a subjective term—it means different things to different people and you'll never satisfy everyone 100%. Instead of fair, he recommends you aim for 'clear and values-driven.'

Clear: whatever formula or criteria or process you agree for working out salaries, make sure it's clear, transparent and everyone understands it.

Values-driven: According to Tom, 'Fairness is an umbrella term, sheltering all sorts of other subjective value-judgements such as meritocracy and equality. You're better off breaking it down and getting clear on what the values really are, and then creating a system based on that.' For example, some people in Tom's former company volunteered to take a pay cut when they saw how much more they were being paid than others. Again, whatever gets agreed should be clear and transparent.

Karin similarly talks about something she calls 'highest level of appropriate engagement' as playing an important role in salary discussions. This refers to how much capacity and energy a person chooses to give the company at a particular point in their life, which varies over time. If you can distinguish the level of engagement and the value a person is actually contributing to the team, it's much richer than calculating salary based on hours or level of experience. Once you decide a process, relate to it as a work in progress and something you can continue to review and adjust based on what's working and what isn't.

Here's an example of a self-managed salary process I learned about from Canadian recruitment firm Fitzii when I interviewed Edwin Jansen, Head of Marketing, for the Leadermorphosis podcast. About a year into their journey to becoming a self-managing organisation, they held a meeting where individuals (then ten people) shared how much they were being paid, how that figure came to be, and how they felt about it. There was a lot of trepidation and anxiety coming into the meeting, but once everything was out in the open, Edwin described it as being almost anticlimactic. Then, Fitzii team members started doing what they call a 'Compensation Advice Process.' Anyone who wants to address their compensation can announce it each quarter, answer a number of pre-decided questions (how they feel about their salary, what is the market rate for that role etc.), and then get advice from their peers (all of which is shared on an online collective decision making platform called Loomio) before the individual makes the final decision about their compensation.

In summary, opening up financial information and self-managing salaries means a much more human and responsive way of working, one which involves:

- A mature and productive working climate, where people can discuss potentially sensitive issues openly, listen to each other, and make decisions together
- Transparency and open access to all information needed to decide salaries, as well as ensuring everyone understands and can make sense of the relevant information
- Committing to an ongoing journey and discovering a compensation model that strives to be clear and values-driven, rather than the umbrella and subjective term 'fair,' incorporating an awareness of each individual's current highest appropriate level of engagement

Deciding salaries together

With the finances now totally open and transparent, it seemed a logical step for the employees to turn their attention to the question of salaries. They agreed that the first step was to decide on what factors the salary would be based. Together they ended up with: years of study or level of education, number of years in this particular field of healthcare, and number of years at Elisabethgården. Since there was a lack of talent in the region, they also decided to pay more than the market average to attract people to the organisation. Out of this a simple rate was created which everyone agreed was fair and clear, enabling employees to easily distinguish their own salary level. When they were recruiting, they could now explain to applicants the rate and the rationale behind it. In one instance, a young woman applied for a position but felt the starting salary was too low. The team member in charge of recruitment (a rotating position) apologised but said this was the rate that had been decided on together and they wouldn't be able to pay any more. She decided to turn the offer down. When the team reflected on this, they realised how important it was to them to hire people who wanted to work here for the mission and not just for the money. 'It was a competitive rate so it's good that she turned us down, otherwise there might have been a conflict in values,' one team member commented.

Financial troubles

Unfortunately, financial troubles began to overshadow our progress and people were, naturally, worried. The nature of the business meant that families would arrive on short notice because of some sort of crisis, so there was always a sense of urgency. Consequently, we were a bit like a fire station – we always needed to be prepared for a call and ready to go and collect a new family. It was impossible to forecast, which we didn't realise when we bought the business. When we were at full capacity, we could turn a healthy profit, but in the beginning, it was never full. Sometimes it was empty for three months and there was nothing you could do about it. When the company is really struggling financially, it's challenging to continue to involve employees because they usually don't have the knowledge or experience of how to deal with it. In this case, no one really had a strong enough interest to upskill themselves or take responsibility for the finances so it meant that the employees weren't able to be involved as much.

At a certain point I realised I was extremely busy with my other businesses and the company needed someone to take it through the financial crises, so my business partner David bought it from us in November 2014. This meant focusing more on the business and less on continuing to coach the team to become self-managing. However, in 2017 it finally turned a profit. David sold the business in November 2017, hoping to move onto something less stressful with more financial stability and resources.

Today, it's doing well and run in a more conventional way. I'm proud of what the team was able to achieve, even in the face of very difficult circumstances. We took a bankrupt company and were able to breathe new life into it, and consequently it has hosted hundreds of families in need over the years and provided valuable support. Perhaps what I'm most proud of is the adult-to-adult dynamic we were able to create between the staff and the clients. Traditionally in health and social care organisations it's easy to fall into a mindset where the caregiver becomes a 'helper,' regarding their clients as more or less helpless. At Elisabethgården our goal was to support the parents who came into our care to become functioning adults in their parenthood, creating the conditions for a sustainable and healthy environment for their children. If the staff began to take care of or compensate for the parents' deficiencies with their own strengths, it wouldn't be conducive to the parents growing and developing for themselves. One example is that the rules and regulations at Elisabethgården used to be communicated to incoming families in a top-down mode, thus defining the relationship dynamic between them as somewhat parent-child, with many parents naturally distrusting or being suspicious of the staff. When we transformed the organisation, this same information was communicated in a totally different way, creating an atmosphere of 'we are all adults here; I have a role to support and empower you and I will regard you as a capable, adult parent. I will be transparent and straightforward and not hide anything from you. I ask you to trust me and to be willing to cooperate for the benefit of your children.'

Summary

- I learned to push for a truly open and straightforward climate and encourage people to be brave, even if the climate seems fairly good or harmonious. Sometimes this means asking people to be open before it feels truly safe, but doing so will create the first building blocks of a safe environment. Self-management will not function over time without the fertile soil of openness.
- There are small signs you can look out for that indicate a self-managing culture is developing, such as someone revealing a hidden skill or interest and taking the lead, or people making decisions involving a large investment without 'asking for permission.' David Marquet in his book 'Turn the Ship Around' calls this the last rung on the ladder of leadership; when an employee goes from 'Tell me what to do' to 'I've done this/I've been doing this.'

- Every sector and every business is different. In Freys, it was a group of young people, curious about new ways of working and with a lot of trust for their manager, Annika, which helped the transformation process. At Komanco and Excosoft, people were really dedicated and engaged in their work, and therefore extremely competent when given the full authority and able to step into their full capacity. At Elisabethgården (and later Mötesbokarna, which you'll learn about in the next story) the employees were more hesitant and were not so confident, which meant it took longer to build trust so people dared to step in.

6. Mötesbokarna: the call centre God forgot

'Power is like fertiliser – in concentrated form it's suffocating, but when distributed it contributes to growth.'

Mats Birgersson, former CEO of Fresh

In August 2012, one of my business partners came back from his holidays excited about a new opportunity his summer house neighbour had told him about. A telemarketing company was up for sale because its founder, who'd been running it for twenty years, wanted to focus on his other business. Intrigued, we drove two and a half hours north of Stockholm to Dalarna to investigate. We learned that the focus of this business was to help companies book customer meetings. It seemed to be well-run with some decent customers. There were eighteen employees – all women – most of whom had worked there for many years. We later jokingly referred to the company as 'the call centre God forgot' because it was as if the clocks had stopped in 1972. There were no computers, everything was recorded on paper, and the decor hadn't been updated for decades.

After months of analysing the business and getting financing from the bank, we signed the papers one snowy day in December. None of the employees knew yet that the business was being sold. Just days before Christmas, after the owner made the announcement, I stepped into the office and addressed the women, who were sat around a large table in the lunchroom. People were in shock and there was an eerie silence in the room. 'My name is Karin Tenelius,' I started, 'and before I say anything else I want to tell you that nothing will happen from now on that you don't agree to. Nothing will be decided without you being involved.' I continued to talk about why we had bought the company, about our ideas and experience with employee-driven, self-managing organisations. After answering some questions for an hour or so, we ended the meeting and set a date to reconvene after the holidays in January. We had agreed that the owner would stay on at the company for a year, mostly because he had managed all the sales and customer relationships. Ordinarily, I would have insisted on a clean break from the previous owner, but we were worried that without this handover period, sales would drop significantly and we needed time to reorganise the sales function.

Ending the reign of fear

In January I spent some days in the office getting to know the staff and navigating the business. I was determined not to become operationally involved as my aim was – as always – to distribute all management responsibilities amongst the team. I was very happy to discover that the two project managers, both women in their late thirties and forties, were very competent. From what I could see, they had responsibility but no authority and they seemed to function more like secretaries to the owner than anything else. They were very used to being managed by him and never making their own decisions. I developed an idea that phase one of the transformation would be to get these two project managers to manage the operations and later, when the rest of the team was ready for more responsibility, we could remove this layer. Since they would be managing other employees, it was essential that these two develop their empowering leadership and coaching skills. I immediately sent them on a four-day leadership training course run by my training company, Tuff, in Stockholm. This training would help them develop the skills they would need to coach the team to become responsible, preventing them from falling into the 'traditional manager traps'. It was very new to them because in all their years of working they had never been on any kind of training. They were nervous about participating in a group with other managers from 'real' companies, people who they thought would be superior and more competent.

This lack of self-esteem was a real pattern amongst the employees. I began to learn that the previous owner had unintentionally established a deeply ingrained culture of management by fear. He had very strict ideas about how things should be and was controlling to the point that everyone was afraid of him. It was his belief that customer calls should be as short as possible and so he monitored everyone's call lengths from his computer. If he noticed something amiss, he'd write a degrading comment on the individual's weekly call statistic sheet and put it in their pigeon-hole messagebox and if that didn't result in an improvement, he would send one of the project managers to complain to the employee who was already feeling low from receiving one of his passive-aggressive notes. One of the project managers shared with me years later that this felt like punishment from behind closed doors, the behaviour of a cowardly dictator.

There was no focus on the quality of the conversations. The sole objective was to make as many calls as possible and get a yes or a no. Consequently, the sales conversion rate was low because it took a lot of calls before a customer meeting was booked. The picture the owner had given us about the staff being quite happy at work seemed very far from reality the more I got to know the business. Employees sat alone in individual, cell-like offices behind closed doors and made calls all day with few breaks. It was tedious work with very little opportunity to grow or develop skills. It was pretty clear that communication rarely ever happened in the open. Most staff meetings were silent but in the corridors, gossip flourished about how miserable everybody was and how bad the boss was.

In the first months I worked with the employees, I listened a lot to all the stories about how constrained, limited and afraid everyone felt. Even though I'd asked the former owner to continue managing the sales function from home until the new sales function was up and running, it became obvious that, like a ghost, his presence was still felt and it was hindering our progress. I realise now it was a mistake to have him stay on at the company as long as twelve months, something I hoped would ease the transition process. In hindsight, it would have been much better to insist he hand everything over on day one to give us a clean slate.

An emaciated business

The big challenge was the working climate. People were happy to agree to having more responsibility and influence but there was low engagement in their actual work. I could understand this, given how uninspiring work had been for them for so long. It was clear that many people worked there because they had no other options rather than because they enjoyed the work. As a result, not everyone was particularly skilled in what they were doing. Although I had a lot of experience training staff in communication, it was hard to crack how we could change this way of executing and perceiving work tasks. To change the whole business model seemed very risky, especially since one of the main reasons for buying the company was that it was already profitable as it was! It's difficult to describe when you know something is wrong but you can't trust your instinct because it's not your trade and you want to respect the twenty years of knowledge and experience in the team.

Knowing what I know now, I could have forced a change much more firmly, both in terms of climate and in terms of the business model. The more I learned about the company, the clearer it became that what small profit it had come from a way of running the business I referred to as 'emaciated.' Overheads were extremely low which is generally a good thing, but not when you consider it an unnecessary luxury to buy pens when people need them! The whole business was a mirror image of the former owner's values. Any costs that benefited employees were always unnecessary and wages were kept as low as possible. I discovered that the wages were barely acceptable and half of the employees were paid by the hour and had been for many, many years. Despite this being illegal, the former owner had created a sort of 'silent agreement' with the union to keep it that way. We knew that paying small salaries and keeping costs so low was not a sustainable way to run the business. Furthermore, I learned that our hourly rate was half of what our competitors were charging so it wasn't profitable either. My sense was this pricing was a reflection of how little value the owner saw in the service his employees offered. He was reluctant to increase the rate and insisted that he always closed the deals – no one but him was involved in pricing discussions with the customers. So little by little, I gave the project managers the authority to not only discuss assignments with customers but to close the deals as well. They quickly became very competent in this, having been directly involved in the work for so many years.

Historically, the previous owner was the only one who had the privilege of seeing the company's finances. Employees knew nothing about how the company was doing in terms of costs and turnover. In order to become a self-managing organisation, I needed to give everyone access to all company information so that everyone could be responsible for its sustainability. One of the project managers in particular was very quick to grasp the financial figures and was very skilled with IT and technology. Incredibly, even though it was 2012, all employees except the project managers and one administrator used pen and paper, no computers! The processes were long winded and so people went through a lot of paper, which had to be copied and filed away in countless binders. We all laugh about it now but it still amazes me how stuck things had been.

Incremental changes

We didn't dare make any large changes as we couldn't risk any significant dips in profitability so we chose to take a safer and slower path. I worked constantly with the employees on the working climate but progress was minimal. People made promises to each other to commit to more straightforward communication but very little changed in the beginning. I also trained people in customer service and some employees adapted to this new way of relating to customers extremely well, which in turn was reflected in the financial results. My experience of this transformation process was that we were driving change slowly and gently. However, when I talked to the team about this period years later, it became clear to me that they had a totally different experience! For them, the change was massive and it happened very quickly. This was a very useful insight for me in understanding how people experience change differently.

In the first six months, we experienced an increase in sales and hoped that the coming autumn would be the right time to make bigger changes that needed to happen like salaries and hiring people on full-time contracts. We promised to make these changes as soon as the company was financially secure. The autumn came but unfortunately, sales had dropped. Our hope had been to increase sales enough that we could keep all 18 employees in employment. In hindsight, this was a big mistake. We didn't succeed in increasing sales and we later discovered that the quality of service we were providing wasn't good enough. Of course, we had several large customers who were satisfied but you could say that they were largely traditional businesses who had fairly low service expectations and were loyal to us because of a long standing relationship. In the rear mirror, I can see that many of the employees weren't suited to this kind of work but it took a long time to spot this because calls were done behind closed doors.

Time for change

For business-related reasons we realised we needed to make some major changes. This new way of working had made it very clear that our image was dusty and old-fashioned. We changed the name of the company and moved to a more modern premises. Our new office space was open plan, which was a drastic departure from the isolated cells of the previous office. This encouraged teamwork and feedback since you could now hear each other's calls. I was there for a day every third week or so and was able to coach people on customer conversations. Being in the same room also made the culture more visible. The first thing that became clear was that the two project managers, although extremely committed, competent and well liked, were struggling to be empowering leaders despite their best intentions. Since people were so helpless, it was a huge challenge to relate to them as capable and hold them to account. As a result, a parent-child culture had emerged with too much pressure on the project managers. For this reason, as well as the fact that we needed to cut down on overheads, we asked one project manager to go back to being a so-called 'communicator.' It also became clear as the weeks went by that one of the employees, the only male, was really struggling with his work. Even with plenty of training, feedback and support, the quality of his calls and his results weren't good enough.

At the same time, I wasn't pleased with the culture overall. I

knew there was still untapped potential in terms of real cooperation. Being such a small team, I could tell there were two
employees who were having a big influence on the dynamic.
Both had a mindset of being 'employed' which made it difficult
for them to adapt to the new, self-managed culture where their
colleagues needed them to act like co-owners of the business.
Despite coaching them a great deal, it became clear that it was
going to take a lot more investment for them to shift their
thinking. I've coached thousands of people with unproductive
mindsets that are stopping them for being successful, so I knew
both had the capacity to change. However, in this situation,
it was impacting the whole culture and it was at a time when
we couldn't afford any setbacks. Ultimately, I had to make the
difficult decision to let these two go. It's always very painful
asking employees to leave but I wanted it to be as respectful and
fair as possible. I spoke to them at the same time and explained
why they were being let go. They were surprised and upset of
course. We paid them for their notice period and they left. One
of them complained to the union but six months later, I heard
he'd found a new job at a Swedish authority and absolutely
loved it, saying that getting sacked was the best thing that could
have happened. He said this new job was perfect for him with
the strict rules and clear instructions of what to do. The rest
of the team was a bit shaken by their departures but to their
surprise, the atmosphere changed over night. Suddenly it was
as if everything was out in the open. If it had been a totally
self-managing culture, of course the team themselves should
have dealt with this problem, but at that time I felt the team's
capacity was not developed enough to deal with such delicate
matters.

Insight #4: Accountability culture – a mindset shift and a skillset upgrade

One of the biggest misconceptions of what it means to be a self-managing organisation is that it's *laissez-faire*, free-for-all, everyone does what they want. The reality couldn't be further from the truth. Amy Edmondson, in researching high performing teams, has a valuable insight to share here in the form of this model:

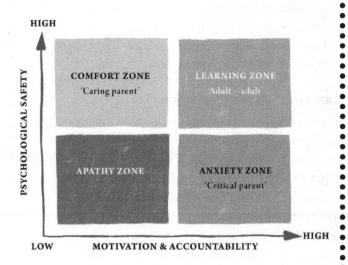

Source: Amy Edmondson's book *Teaming*

Edmondson tells us that fostering a culture of both high psychological safety *and* high motivation and accountability is key to an effective team. Too much of the former results in a 'Comfort Zone' culture where people might feel safe, but not challenged, and feedback isn't really happening. I've added the distinction here of 'caring parent' to describe the leadership

dynamic that's often at play in this zone, where leaders are usually overly protective or 'nice'. And of course, too much motivation and accountability without psychological safety isn't
good either and creates an atmosphere of fear and anxiety. Here
I've added the label 'critical parent' to describe the leadership
dynamic of leaders not trusting people, stepping in, criticising,
punishing and so on.

In theory, this all sounds logical but in practice, operating
in the 'Learning Zone' – where we relate to each other in an
adult-to-adult way in a partnership-style culture – is another
thing entirely. It requires a mindset shift, a skillset upgrade and
a great deal of daily commitment.

A mindset shift from 'power over' to 'power with'

Many organisations in the initial stages of becoming self-managed slip into the 'Comfort Zone'. Traditional organisations
tend to enforce accountability through coercion – incentives
and punishments, carrots and sticks. In a self-managing team
or organisation, we all become jointly accountable for 1) the
health of the organisation, and 2) the health of the team. This
is, again, a mindset shift, primarily in terms of how we relate
to power. American social worker turned management theorist
Mary Parker Follett was writing about types of power as early
as the 1920s. She distinguished between coercive power, or 'power
over', and the jointly developed coactive power, or 'power with.'
She believed it's not possible to get rid of power over – it's a natural
human tendency, but it's good to try and reduce it. This takes
a lot of unlearning and relearning on both the part of former
managers or leaders and former employees or non-leaders (who
have been conditioned to adopt a 'power under' mindset and way

of being – a bit passive, waiting for the leaders to decide or act, being overly adaptable or tolerant).[1]

Creating accountability for the health of the organisation

In terms of creating the conditions for everyone to feel jointly accountable for the health of the company, Frederic Laloux suggests three ingredients for creating a self-correcting system in a self-managing organisation.[2]

1. **Psychological ownership** of the organisation, of the work – if people don't care about the organisation's mission or their work, don't introduce self-management prematurely

2. **Everyone in the organisation must directly experience the outcome of their work and actions** – in other words, everyone directly feels the pain and pride that comes from their work which you can achieve by:

a. Creating *norms* of what healthy or good looks like, for example, in a team

b. Ensuring a regular stream of *feedback* or *data* to know how you're doing

c. Making space for *conversations* where you can share what you sense, look at the data and look at the tension or opportunity

3. **Everyone has the power to make changes** – if I feel the pain of something not working, I need to be able to take action

1 See also the whitepaper *Pathways to partnership – looking down and looking up behaviours* (1995) by Bob Anderson, Founder and CEO of The Leadership Circle, about 'looking down' and 'looking up' behaviours.

2 See Frederic Laloux's 'Insights for the Journey' video 'Understanding self-correcting systems' here: https://thejourney.reinventingorganizations. com/4111.html

using, for example, the advice process, without needing to first seek approval

Of course a prerequisite of these three ingredients is transparency and open sharing of information such as company financial data, as we've previously shared.

Creating accountability for the health of the team

As for people coactively maintaining the health of the team (or teams), this is again a mindset shift from 'team health is the manager or HR's responsibility' to 'each one of us is responsible for and can influence the team's health.' We've already talked about the Cooperation Coaching and 'moose heads' practices as tools for building a team's capacity to name and shift their working climate. Dialogues about team health can be anything from discussing a missed deadline, to inviting a colleague to leave the organisation. Almost all of these conversations are tough, both because most of us haven't learned how to hold them effectively, and because our brains are wired to avoid conflict so it takes some practice and intent to lean into them with compassion and commitment.

Here are some starting points that can help you on this journey:

- Skills training (for example in giving feedback, being radically honest, transforming conflicts, some form of nonviolent communication, integrative decision making and so on)
- Create (safe) spaces for conversations to name tensions or gaps in accountability and together find ways forward

- Offer coaches to teams who struggle with this
- Learn about examples of accountability practices in other self-managing organisations such as Morning Star's 'Colleague Letter of Understanding' (an agreement each person makes with their peers regarding their goals and commitments to each other) or Wellbeing Teams' 'Confirmation Statements' (a set of statements about what would be true if an individual or team were achieving their purpose, which helps individuals and teams to hold each other, with the help of a coach, to account)
- Cocreate a clear conflict engagement system (see this example by self-managing collective Enspiral in their open source handbook: https://handbook.enspiral.com/guides/conflict-resolution.html)

New level of financial literacy

Over time, I began to notice two promising signs that self-management was really starting to blossom. First, when I came into the office (at this point, maybe once every three weeks), people greeted me but didn't stop their work or pay too much attention. Before, everyone would stop what they were doing when I arrived, as if it was me 'carrying' the business. The second indicator was noticing that in coffee and lunch breaks, people were still engaged in talking about their work. Of course, there's nothing wrong with chit-chat and talking about things besides work is important too, but in my experience, self-managing teams naturally want to talk about work in breaks, whereas teams in many traditional, hierarchical organisations tend to talk about anything that will help them avoid the drudgery of work.

113

The team had become highly responsible for their customers and with this new culture of openness, people could really start to engage with the finances and the business results we needed for the company to become profitable. One example of the team taking an interest was that they questioned what they were able to charge for billable time. Where did the hours go? What were they doing with them? My business partner and I supported the team in setting a target of 80% billable time, and they all agreed this seemed like an appropriate metric. At one meeting someone came up with the idea of tracking their time. 'We can trial it for four weeks so we have some actual data,' she suggested. The project began at once. After a few weeks, it was much clearer to everyone how they were spending their time and almost automatically their rate went up. People felt more secure having this as a routine, knowing that these targets were meaningful in the context of the sustainability of their business.

Everyone a recruiter

Everyone became responsible for recruitment and onboarding. I wasn't even asked to meet the applicants but I trusted the team implicitly to know what skills and mindset were essential in order to thrive in the working environment we had created. The team became extremely picky about who they felt was a good fit. We even wrote a 'scare them away' letter to give to those considering the job before they accepted the offer:

'Scare them away' letter

For you to consider before accepting our job offer

In a small company organised the way we are, the traditional employer-employee relationship is replaced with a partnership. This means that:

- You cannot expect the same service, support and infrastructure as you would in a larger organisation. This means the things you miss might need to be initiated and created by you.
- You are regarded as someone who is really important in terms of how our company is doing, not just as someone who comes in and does their job.
- You will have more responsibility for the whole picture, and you will also be able to have a greater impact than in a larger organisation.
- You will feel a bit more insecure than you might in a larger organisation. How the company is doing financially has a more direct correlation to your employment.
- The owners will work together with you but they will not manage the company – you and your colleagues will.
- You will be required to contribute and take initiative. You will have to adapt to the fact that not everything will be in place, taken care of or running perfectly.
- To work in this way, open and straightforward communication is essential. This is a strong part of our culture.

All of us have different needs and desires in our workplaces where we spend a great deal of our lives. It is worth considering yours – what do you want from your future workplace?

From experience we know that it takes more to work in a small business versus a larger one with its resources and established systems. We ask you to think about this and see if you are a match with us.

The shift to becoming a self-managing organisation resulted in team members becoming responsible, engaged and skilled communicators who produced great results for our customers. Customers were giving us positive feedback and recommending us. The telemarketing sector has a bad reputation so one of our biggest challenges in sales was to listen to the customer's scepticism and ask them to let us show how we could offer something different. Out of this, a vision for the company began to emerge, something bigger than the day-to-day work we were doing. Booking meetings for our customers' salesforce helped our customers with their sales figures, of course. But the employees, who had never really had a passion for telemarketing itself, became invested in creating a workplace where people can do great work and have the freedom to be mental owners of the business with their colleagues.

The self-esteem of individuals grew each day. People had a new pride in their job which was miles away from what they had felt before. Complaints about 'the old company' had been that it was monotonous and dull calling people all day. Everyone wished they could do something else and snatched any opportunity to do any other task. Whereas now, people told me, 'Every day is different and we are involved in everything.' Just before Christmas that year, we had a gathering to close the season and I asked, 'What highlight would you like to share from this year?' One of the shyest members of the team surprised us by speaking up. 'I'll start! I just want to say that my highlight is that I am so proud of what we have all accomplished together. This is a totally new company and we have all created it.'

A blind spot revealed

At last, things were running as they should be – we had a self-managing organisation with a healthy working climate in place. Or so I thought. As it happened, we had one more level to go. My presence had long since become unnecessary for the running of day-to-day business so I only visited the company once in awhile to facilitate quarterly meetings or to train employees in customer conversations. For this reason, I was blind to a phenomenon that was preventing the team being completely self-managing. Well, we were about to get a rude awakening.

One of the former project managers, Jennie, was extremely competent, particularly in all things technology-related. Her skills and reliability made her a natural leader and others leaned on her for support. We all knew this, of course, but we didn't realise the full extent of this dependency. Over the years I had been regularly coaching her to develop more of a healthy, balanced workload. It's always harder to be meticulous about coaching employees when they are so capable. It's convenient to allow them to take responsibility because it helps you step out of the way. Jennie would never complain and would just plough ahead. But by the middle of February in 2016, it was clear she had reached a breaking point and needed to make some serious changes. We all understood that this would take time and we gave her all the support she needed. One of her teammates, Ylva, reflected on this period:

> First, it was kind of a shock when she left. And yet, I knew it was coming – you could tell for years it was going to happen. My first thought was 'How will we manage this now? What's possible?' But just after a few days, we saw that we were able to solve problems together. It's even more fun to work now and you have even more insights so it's sort of good for the company! But at the same time, it was sad that she wasn't here. At first, I thought 'This is not gonna work. We should close the company down now.' But that wasn't the case. So it's a roller-coaster! There are no normal days or weeks.

Back in the office, it was amazing to see that there was still potential waiting to be liberated. Everyone grew immensely and learned a lot in the following weeks as they picked up all the responsibilities that she had been silently hoarding – writing proposals to potential customers, mastering the IT systems, tracking the business figures. Many of these things had been in the pipeline for the wider team to learn about but had been put off. Now there was a real and pressing need to learn them!

What happened next

Although together we created a completely different work-place, sadly we never succeeded in achieving truly great business results. It became clear that we really needed to invest significantly in service development and hiring new people with greater technical expertise. It was also becoming clear that the industry was shifting – suppliers and buyers were finding each other in more efficient ways than meetings set up as a result of cold calling. To stay in the game, we would need to reinvent the whole business model. We explored the option of selling the business, but many of our competitors shared they were struggling with the same challenges – this industry's days were numbered. In the end, we decided to close the business in April 2017. My business partner and I had bought the company driven by a passion to create a great workplace rather than an interest or expertise in telemarketing, but sadly this was not enough to meet the future demands of this sector.

I was truly moved and touched by the dignity and the lack of blame I experienced when we had the final discussions about the future of the company with the team. Everyone was already aware of the financial situation and so it was no shock that we had reached such final terms. Of course that didn't diminish the grief and sadness everyone felt, but the team continued to work together until the end. There was no trace of the helplessness and resignation I encountered when I first visited the company when we had bought it nearly four and a half years ago.

Almost a year after we shut the business down I had a long phone conversation with Jennie, who is now studying to become an HR manager so that she can 'spread this way of working to other organisations.' One thing we reflected on together is how important it is in a self-managing organisation to have people who are doing 'their thing.' In Komanco and Excosoft, it was clear that all of the employees really loved their work so there was no issue. Whereas with Mötesbokarna, this was not the case. When we took over, many employees had stayed on for many years even though they resented the work itself and the management. Once we began the transformation process, people became much more engaged in creating an engaging workplace, rather than the work itself. In pyramidal hierarchies, it isn't such a problem if people do work they aren't passionate about because there are a lot of rules and controls in place. However, in a self-managing organisation people need to truly care about the work in order to drive the business forward because no one else is responsible for doing this.

The other huge revelation was hearing how people had moved on since leaving the company, many in unexpected directions. We talked and talked about many people who had taken big steps, not only in their careers, but also in their lives such as getting divorced or moving cities. It suddenly struck me: if we looked at it from a business perspective; we failed – there's no question about that. But what if we look at it through another lens? Imagine that instead of buying a company, we had been given an assignment by a state authority or the EU to develop these people and their employment was just the context for their training ground. I don't say this to conceal the fact that we failed business-wise, but rather because it's clear to me that self-management is a powerful way to give people the opportunity to develop and grow. Looking back, perhaps we should have sat down with the team early on and reinvented the business from scratch with a new product or service that was more inspiring to the individuals.

Summary

- With Mötesbokarna, I learned that it's helpful to make an early statement about two values that will not be up for negotiation: that the organisation will be run by self-managing principles and that the climate will be developed to consist of honesty, openness, and straightforward communication. This way, it's easier for people to make decisions about whether they want to continue or leave.

- When moving to a culture of transparency and responsibility, it becomes visible fairly quickly which employees are competent and which lack the skills needed to be successful, many times because they have landed in the wrong profession. Quite often the solution is to support the employee to find a job that better aligns with their needs and purpose – something they tend to be very grateful for.

- One of my favourite benefits of developing a self-managing organisation is that the company becomes more resilient because everyone, not just the CEO or owner, has a shared mental ownership of the business. When market disruptions or crises occur, the whole team springs into action to find solutions and adapt. It is like a bunch of business partners taking care of their company instead of passive employees wondering what is happening and waiting to be rescued.

- I have seen time and time again that the people involved in the transition to a self-managing organisation grow exponentially. Even if the company fails, it isn't experienced as a catastrophe because of the self-esteem and new breadth and depth of skills people have developed, making it much easier to find new jobs.

7. Tuff Leadership Training: pulling it all together

The final story I want to share is what we have learned from creating a company from scratch as a self-managing organisation. I founded Tuff Leadership Training together with Carl Erik Herlitz in 2003. We decided to start the company based on two fundamental ideas. First, we wanted to use my experiences with Freys Hotel and Komanco and share the knowledge to support others who were interested in working in more self-managing ways. Second, we were convinced that the leadership skills needed for this could only be developed through practical training. Our mission would be to create human workplaces by helping organisations discover a better way to lead, one which liberates people's full power and potential. We called the company Tuff Leadership Training ('Tuff' being the Swedish word for 'tough') because we knew the training would be intense and challenging. It was a big risk starting yet another leadership training consultancy because it was, and still is, an overpopulated sector with lots of competition. But we were up for the challenge and prepared to wait a long time for us to become established. Of course we didn't realise just how long it would take in the end.

Rough beginnings

Before we officially founded the company, we created a small network of people with shared values who really liked our methodology. We had regular meetings in the basement of our house in Täby, outside of Stockholm. In the beginning, there were six of us who started by offering open courses. For a long time, our only participants were friends and family. In the end, it took around ten years to reach a level of turnover where everyone involved could make a living out of the work we did. Looking back, it's quite amazing that we all hung in there. The main reason it took so long was that we were much too early with our concept in Sweden. We mostly spoke to HR professionals and back then, everyone was more or less happy with the quality of leadership in their companies. The common picture in Sweden was: 'We are the world champions in involving leadership and we have no pain points.' As a team, we had frequent meetings discussing if we should continue or not because it was so hard to get through to anyone with our offer. Fortunately, we had a few customers we could call fans, many of whom are still with us today, and the impact we could see we were making kept us going.

Perpetual learning

During all these years of struggling, we used the time for intense training. We, the founders, always had the vision that the role of the trainers was not to transmit theoretical knowledge, but to cause real shifts, both in course participants and customer organisations. Very early on, our trainers scored excellent ratings from our customers, but as founders, we knew there was even greater potential to be reached. Four or five years in, we had a big discussion at one of our company retreats in which trainers raised the issue that Carl Erik and I 'were never content' and complained, 'aren't the customer ratings sufficient?' Of course I agreed the trainers were highly skilled, but I stood for the potential still available for causing shifts which is hard to grasp if you've never really experienced this. We also re-emphasised our commitment to continuous learning in order to benefit our customers even more. Today, we still have this habit so that no matter how masterful and experienced you are as a consultant, you train with your colleagues once a month.

Leadership lessons as founders

Traditionally as a founder, you can unilaterally decide to go in a certain direction. At Tuff, however, our ambition was always to do things together. There were challenging moments that tested this from the beginning. For example, in the early years we would often discuss if we should do 'a little bit of everything' as a consultancy, since the demand for training in leadership skills for less hierarchical ways of working was close to zero back then. Carl Erik and I had very strong opinions about sticking to our niche expertise, in spite of the lack of demand, since this was our true mission. We were a group of people with diverse skills and experience, many with different ideas about what to offer, including everything from presentation skills training to couples counselling. It was important to us not to dictate our mission and so it tested our ability to create engagement for ideas and truly listen to people so they felt heard, without using our power to coerce or convince people. Today it's all long forgotten and everyone is clear on our unique strength and offering as a company.

As a person with strong opinions, there have been many times when I've been prepared to fight for my ideas because I know they won't happen unless they get full approval from the group. Over time I've learnt to give up some of my ideas and I've found they sometimes ripen as time goes by and suddenly there is energy for them further down the line. A lot of this is about practicing being patient, and reminding myself of the principles of concordance.

Building on what you have

I had hoped that creating my own company from scratch meant that I could create a fully self-managing organisation from day one. So it was frustrating and puzzling to me when this didn't go as planned. Looking back now, I see several reasons for this. One is that we had recruited people who were very skilled trainers, consultants and coaches but less interested in the business development part. An issue that bothered me for years was people's lack of interest in the company finances. Our finances are totally open and transparent and we tried endless solutions to create joint responsibility for keeping the company in good shape profit-wise but nothing stuck. In the end, I had to face the reality that my colleagues just weren't motivated by or interested in learning about figures. This was surprising because I previously hadn't had any problems engaging employees with the finances in the companies I had helped transform.

On the plus side, it's clear that no one is motivated solely by money at Tuff. People are here to make a difference, and to do great work. So I let go of trying to generate engagement and we decided to hire Marlena to manage the finances, someone who loves curling up with a book on the latest accounting rules. It's been great for us to be able to focus on the things we're passionate about and good at.

Something else that was missing for a long time at Tuff was what we call 'project power.' I had a tendency to try and make people drive projects that needed to be managed and longed for colleagues that were as interested in business development as I was. For example, many times I brought up a desire to expand Tuff's services into Europe but never quite got the enthusiasm I was looking for. Eventually, I realised I didn't have to force anyone to help me with this initiative and instead asked the group for the mandate for me to take ownership of this project. They said yes, and I was so relieved! Fortunately for me, we have two new additions to the team who are both interested in sales and have finally brought project power into the mix.

The lesson this has taught me is about building on people's talents and passions rather than forcing them into something the company badly needs. Self-management doesn't mean that everyone has to do everything. We can still have different roles, specialities and interests. I've learnt that it's better to recruit for something that's missing than to try imposing it on people who aren't interested. Of course, this doesn't mean avoiding challenges. Quite the opposite. We have a strong feedback culture where colleagues will always bring your pitfalls up, or highlight a potential that you might be blind to.

Culture of development

Something that we wanted to create from the beginning was a culture of development. We contribute to each other every day and we also have whole-company offsites twice a year which tend to be focused either entirely or mostly on personal development. One framework we use in our courses and also with each other at Tuff is Daniel Ofman's 'Core Quality Quadrant.'

Insight #5: Core Quality Quadrant

Daniel Ofman, a management coach from the Netherlands, developed the Core Quality Quadrant to help people 'turn reactivity into creativity.' At the centre of the model is the notion that we all have a number of core qualities from a young age, such as determination, flexibility, or cheerfulness. To take an example, let's say a Core Quality you have is *flexibility*. Sometimes you might overplay this quality, making it too much of a good thing and end up, having *fickleness*. This is your Pitfall. (Ofman uses the language 'having' a Core Quality or a Pitfall, rather than 'being' it.) Your challenge, then, is the positive opposite of your pitfall and also preferably something you are inspired by. In this case, it might be *consistency*. Too much of your challenge, though, and it is your Allergy – that which you can't stand in other people. In this instance, it might be *rigidity*.

Ofman tells us that the most important thing your core quadrant tells you is that it's all about finding the balance between your quality and your challenge. It's not either/or but both/and. So in terms of our personal development, we can choose to train in and practice our Challenge, and even learn from the people who have too much of our Challenge and trigger our Allergy.

(Read 'Fancy Meeting Me Here! Discovery Your Core Qualities' by Daniel Ofman or visit https://corequality.nl/ if you're interested in learning more.)

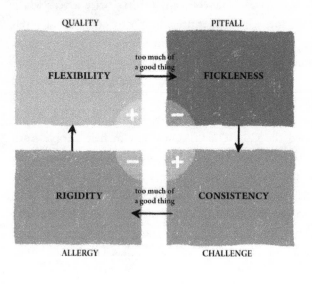

At Tuff, we work a lot with our core quadrants and explore them at our offsites or in coaching sessions. It's really useful in terms of nurturing a feedback culture because we can give each other feedback when we are having our Pitfall and help each other practice our Challenge. One of my Core Qualities, as you might have guessed by now, is drive. My colleagues (and husband!) have told me that when I overplay my Quality, I'm like a bulldozer. Giving my Pitfall a nickname like bulldozer helps us all communicate in shorthand so whenever I fall into that trap, people can call me out. My Challenge is to slow down. And of course my allergy is inaction.

I remember at one point, my drive had resulted in making some investments on behalf of the company that in hindsight were a bit too risky. A lot of questions were raised about my judgment and whether I was reliable in estimating risks. Things weren't going as planned and the fear of losing money and people's livelihood stirred up a lot of heated debates. However, the fact that we were able to go through these storms and restore the confidence and trust in our relationships meant we came out on the other side much stronger. The stormy weather included being very, very honest about what we really thought of each other in our darkest moments. I, for instance, had to deal with being regarded as not trustworthy, which is something I find really difficult because my strong suit is being reliable. When something we value about ourselves is called into question, it stirs up emotions and we tend to become defensive, revealing our vulnerable, sensitive core. At Tuff, we all know what each other's five year-old version of themselves looks like by now and it's almost impossible to hide this inner child here. We give each other lots of support to be able to take care of the inner five year-old in order to act less out of fear and more out of choice. You won't be able to get away with letting your five year-old self-dominate for long because that would be lovingly intolerable.

One of our values is about caring for each other and we say: 'We are totally ok with you – everything that makes you human – and at the same time, we relate to you as your potential – the bigger you, the unique talent you might not see yourself (or want to see. We will listen to you and acknowledge all your thoughts, feelings and needs and we will pay attention to your steps ahead, big and small. At the same time – with a lot of listening, respect and love – we will be frank about what we see beneath the surface and challenge that which we think is keeping you stuck. We will say these things even when we don't want to, when it would be much easier not to, and we say it even when you might not want to hear it; when it might hurt.'

How we've evolved

Nowadays, we have four full-time, back office employees who are totally self-managed. In practice, this means they have no manager and are free to work when, how and where they want. For example, Kajsa (whose role encompasses managing courses, company information and the office), once worked from Senegal for three months. Our finance wizard, Marlena, started with us as an intern after moving to Sweden from Poland. Before Tuff, she worked for a large company in Gdansk for eight years. In the beginning, she didn't dare sit with us at the lunch table since she regarded us as managers, and she sometimes still tells me, 'I think I want to take some time off on Thursday or Friday.' I remind her she doesn't need to tell me and she knows this but she does it anyway. It's hard for her to break these habits, even after six years, but we laugh about it. She says, 'I've stopped telling people back in Poland about my job here because they think I'm lying!'

We have around sixteen consultants working for Tuff who also choose how much they work. When people have children, for example, they often choose to scale back their hours for a while. As long as the team is happy and the company is healthy, you can steer your own work. Of course, it doesn't work if everyone goes on holiday in the same week so we have made agreements to consider each other in the same way we would a member of our family. You wouldn't suddenly decide to go to Italy for two weeks without asking your spouse, for example! We often do this on Slack, checking with people before we book something. There are no exact rules, really, because it's self-regulating – people need to support themselves so naturally they won't just go on holiday all the time.

A transparent, fair financial system has evolved over the years, which distributes the resources to everyone involved based on each person's specific contribution, and makes sure the company is robust enough. If something in the system isn't quite working, or circumstances change, it's very easy to adjust. There's no management team, and though we have a CEO (me) and a board (filled by a few of the Tuff team) on paper for legal reasons, neither the CEO or the board has any formal power. If everyone agrees to change our system, we do. At the end of each year, we design a bonus, if there is room for one, and agree on it together. Since we don't believe in bonuses as motivators, it's more natural to decide from year to year. Up to this point, we have divided bonuses equally among us, since that felt right.

Decision-making

We practice concordance decision making (outlined in Chapter 1) at Tuff and have agreed that big decisions involve everybody, but not all decisions are made together. Decisions concerning

131

the office, for example, are made by the people who spend the most time there or have the most interest in it. Kajsa and one of our consultants, David, are interested and invested in the office interior design so they take the lead on that. Recently we felt a need to reorganise into teams with agreed responsibilities as it was becoming inefficient having regular all-company meetings whose decisions didn't concern everyone. We now have a consulting team, a research and development team, a marketing and social media team, and a strategy team who meet however often is useful for them. And we have a whole-company offsite twice a year.

Our principle of organising is trial and error. I couldn't tell you, for example, how many models we have tried over the years – some last and some need to adapt as we grow. To the outside world, our way of organising might seem inefficient or chaotic compared to the formal organisational charts many people are used to. However, having this fluid, self-correcting structure has enabled us to be really efficient and lean with no energy wasted – nothing slips through the cracks and our customers give us high scores in terms of reliability. There is no one person orchestrating or controlling anything. People I speak to in future of work communities often get upset about anything that starts to resemble a hierarchy in a self-managing organisation. However, I believe that leaders will always emerge in different areas and it makes sense to acknowledge this and make it visible rather than resist it. At Tuff, we all happily give people the mandate to make decisions on areas where they have the most expertise and interest. Recently I interviewed Mats Birgersson, who transformed a ventilation equipment manufacturing company in Sweden to a thriving self-managing organisation in the nineties, and he had this fitting quote: 'Power is like fertiliser – in concentrated form it's suffocating, but when it's distributed it contributes to growth.'

> 'I think it's important to say that it's not that everything is always fun or easy or happy. But the difference is that there is always space for everything; for all parts of ourselves. It's not that everything is lovey dovey and we're always friends. But if there is something, we can talk about it and there's always space to develop and for everything to be as it is. Not everything is perfect, it's not a perfect world. And it takes courage to talk about what needs to be talked about. It's not really normal in Swedish culture. So everyone needs to be a bit groundbreaking. The truth is more important than looking good. We all need to contribute to changing a bad working environment; it's not just up to the boss because we don't have one.'
>
> Kajsa Thelander Sadio, Tuff Leadership Training

The joys and frustrations of working in a self-managing organisation

If you ask anyone at Tuff (and I'd wager most self-managing organisations) what they value the most, they'd tell you it's the freedom. Freedom to be themselves, to work how and when they want. But with great freedom comes great responsibility. I think of self-managing organisations like the Internet of Things – every employee becomes a culture sensor, responsible for constantly sending and receiving data about how the climate is in the group. In the story about Komanco, I shared the 'moose head' tool. Almost all of our meetings at Tuff start with the question, 'Does anyone have any moose heads?' and after years of practicing, it's still tough and uncomfortable to bring up moose heads with each other. Our brains are wired for social safety so training to override this in service of creating an open and straightforward climate takes real grit. But we all know that if we don't make the effort, the culture will clog up; uncertainty will root, trust will erode, and uncommunicated complaints will start to itch and affect our efficiency.

Another one of our values is 'We want everything to be said, always.' It goes like this:

We understand the value of being able to and being allowed to say it how it is – everything from the big things, to the tiniest things. Openness is crucial for our business, for our relationships, for trust, and for continuously developing. We know that what's not out in the open can't shift – not in us, and not between us. Sometimes we struggle with the fear of not looking good or appearing critical or pathetic but we also know that our smallness and our feelings are always allowed to be and that we all welcome these feelings to be named. We know that it takes courage to admit doubts, worries and being wrong, and having an environment that really encourages this is fundamental for our work. We also promise to say if there's something, big or small, that's irritating us – something that's not complete or ready – because we know that inauthenticity and pretending everything is fine is always in the way of healthy relationships, creativity, true cooperation and everything we want to accomplish.

This kind of commitment and level of communication also demands constant personal development. Our consultants train particularly hard in this because they need to model it to all of our course participants and clients. Only in the last two years has there been a shift in our discussions from the 'Why are you never content, Karin and Carl Erik?!' to 'We accept that training constantly is beneficial.' In a recent consultant training session, Eva shared that for her, part of the mindset shift happened when he stopped calling it 'training' and instead began calling it 'development.'

David Valentin's story

Ever since I was a child, I've struggled with a fear of performing, of needing to 'seem smart.' This has also showed up in my time as a course leader at Tuff. It's often challenging for me to take a stand, to believe I have the expertise and to be committed to another person's development, daring to challenge that person's worldview. It's also not unusual for course participants to react defensively to the content of the courses. If I'm in a bad place in terms of my self-confidence, these situations are even more challenging.

For a while I thought this was so difficult that I didn't think it was worth it. I slept badly the night before a course, I had trouble eating, I struggled to gather the motivation to lead a really good course. I longed for a job that didn't require so much of me as a person, a job where I could perform tasks someone else created and then go home and be free, not having to worry about tomorrow. After a lot of reflection, I decided to try something else. I talked to my colleagues and they understood, they had seen me struggle and in many cases coached me about my challenges. I applied for a job as a salesman and got it.

At first it was fun learning new things and I had fairly low expectations of myself because I was the new guy. It was also nice to have a 9-to-5 job I didn't bring home. But as time went by, I felt like something was missing. At first I ignored these thoughts but after almost a year in the new job, I called Karin. I told her how I felt and asked if we could talk about if it could be possible for me to come back to Tuff.

I've been back at Tuff for a year now. It's been a tough year and I've been wrestling a lot with my fears. Strangely enough, it doesn't feel as tough as it was before I took my 'sabbatical.' I think the act of really choosing this job again meant I no longer struggled with the unproductive mindset that 'it shouldn't be like this.' It's given me more determination to endure difficult moments. As a result, I take more risks and create situations where I can be really proud of myself and Tuff. It contributes to a stronger self-confidence and slowly but surely I can do more to be of service to others, rather than trying to impress people. I'm very happy, both because I dared to try something new, but mostly because I dared to come back and try again.

What's next?

For me, the great thing about creating a self-managing or-ganisation is that Tuff is not at all reliant or dependant on me being a traditional CEO. Mostly, it's just a title we have to put on a form to satisfy state authorities (and it's sometimes useful to exercise this power when on the phone to suppliers!). Of course, I'm passionate about the work we do so I engage in it, and when I do I choose what I like doing best. Today this mostly involves networking, giving talks on self-managing organisations, developing new services, expanding into new markets, and I still coach the consultants, although Carl Erik is the main source for this. My best practice, which I use constantly, is to ask, 'Who could do this?' If the answer is 'no one but me' (which is very rare), then I consider doing it myself. Although I have a lot of drive, I'm also quite lazy – I'm not someone who finishes reading books and I'm much more interested in generating ideas than executing the minute details. I often think being lazy is a helpful trait if you're interested in being an empowering leader.

I'm also happy that Tuff has finally been able to 'come out of the closet'. We used to be shy about our organisational self-management experience because in the beginning, it scared away our customers. Now we've updated our website and we can finally be proud and open about our expertise in this area because there's a growing appetite for us to support organisations in becoming self-managing and it's no longer perceived as totally radical by our customers in more traditional organisations. They may not want to go fully self-managed, but they appreciate the benefits of a more involving, coaching leadership style that we can offer their managers the chance to develop. I'm excited that we've started working with some small and medium organisations who want to partner with us over three years to become fully self-managing and to develop the mindset, leadership and culture aspect of this.

But something that I've been sitting with for a while now is: How can we impact people beyond the corporate world, people with less privilege? We already lead a lot of Step 1 courses for teachers in schools up and down Sweden because the same adult-adult, coaching mindset and way of being applies to the teacher-student relationship i.e. how can you empower children who have to go to school by law to really *choose* to participate in school, and ultimately to be the authors of their own lives? We also offer our Cooperation Coaching and other services to schools like Glömstaskolan, which Lisa has blogged about because of its radical approach to rules and brilliant support systems for children with Special Educational Needs. However, I'd like to explore how we can be doing more.

Part 3
Tips for fellow travellers

8. Some thoughts for you about the journey

We hope you've found the stories and insights in this book useful so far. As we wrote in the beginning, this isn't a handbook but we would like to support people in creating and self-managing organisations, especially the mindset, leadership and culture part. This section of the book is intended to give you some starting points and a sense of what the journey might look like, based on what we've learned over the years.

In Chapters 1 to 4, we identified three pillars for developing an effective self-managing team or organisation which are: 1) a coaching mindset and way of being; 2) a focus on working climate; and 3) a culture of mandate and involvement. An overview of the journey to becoming self-managing, then, could look like on the opposite page.

This means moving from a parent-child to adult-adult dynamic, from the manager or leader being responsible, to the team being responsible. We've also found it incredibly powerful to train our ability to talk about what's underneath the surface – feelings, emotions, ways of being, mindsets – and to tackle these

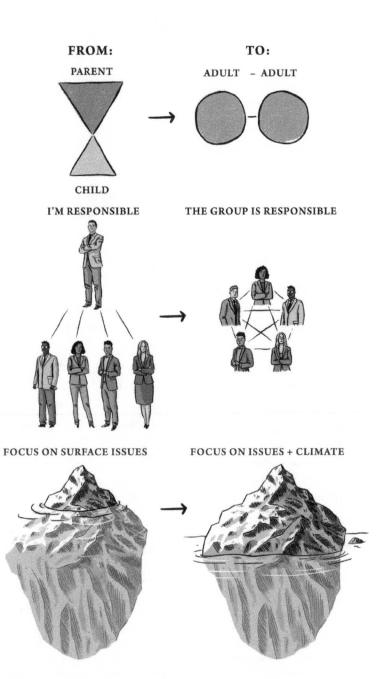

things first before addressing surface or operational issues. This way you have a productive, open and trustful climate on top of which you can solve just about any problem together.

How to start: get the mandate

There's no one right way to start the journey to self-management, of course. However, in our experience, it's crucial to get the mandate for the transformation from the whole organisation or team. Spanish consultancy K2K Emocionando, for example, makes sure there is 100% buy-in from the owners and CEO of the company before they start a transformation process. After that, they close the company for two days and give employees the opportunity to visit other organisations that have transformed to self-management before giving them the chance to vote for change. Only if 80% of employees vote 'yes' for the transformation do K2K actually go ahead with it.[3]

The benefits of having people choose the change are huge. Working in a self-managed, adult-adult way only works if people have a shared ownership of the process and for the company itself. In our opinion, many self-management experiments fail because it's imposed on people from above rather than truly chosen. So to help people choose, consider what's most useful for them to know and make space for people to ask lots of questions.

In terms of how much to say and what to say, we agree with Frederic Laloux that using jargon like 'self-management' is perhaps not the best way to go. He says 'always try to put story

3   See this Corporate Rebels article for more about K2K: https://corporate-rebels.com/ner-group/

over concept,' even if that story is just half a sentence. For example, you might say that you're interested in shifting how you work together ..:

> '... for everyone to be powerful... for teams to own their own decisions ... because I no longer want to impose targets top down ... to avoid lengthy approval mechanisms ... because there is more intelligence in 100 heads than in one ... (and so on).[4]'

As I (Karin) said in Chapter 6, I think it's helpful to make an early statement about two non-negotiables: 1) that the organisation will be run by self-managing principles (*i.e.* power and authority will be distributed); and 2) that the climate will be developed to consist of honesty, openness, and straightforward communication.

What next?

Once you have the mandate, our advice is to start having dialogues that lead to choice, which then lead to ownership and responsibility. Start talking about the working climate in a team. Get the team to be responsible for making agreements about creating a working climate that works for them. Start talking about how we're going to make decisions now there's no longer a boss. Start talking about who is going to take care of the former managers' responsibilities. All the time, place the responsibility with the team or the individual.

4   See Frederic Laloux's 'Insights for the Journey' video 'Use the term self-management?' here: https://thejourney.reinventingorganizations. com/422.html

How to know when it's working

One of the most striking things you'll notice when you visit a self-managing organisation or team is the sense of engagement. It's not the kind of stock photo, smiling professionals-type engagement, but rather periods of silent concentration, animated conflict transformation, lots of open and straightforward communication, people taking charge of their meetings. If you're a former manager, especially a founder or CEO, a good sign that self-management is taking hold is when you stumble across a decision-making meeting you weren't invited to, or people paying little attention when you arrive in the office, or observe people claiming their leadership to resolve a challenge without looking to you for guidance. It can be a strange feeling to no longer be needed in the old, heroic leader-archetype sense. Of course, you'll still have roles to play, but you're no longer the person everyone looks to by default to solve or approve things. Johan Lassing, from a self-managing IT company in Sweden, calls this the lighthouse effect. It's impossible not to be drawn to the light like moths, even when you've been given 'permission' to make your own decisions. But when you turn the lighthouse off, magical things happen.

If at any point you start to panic and think 'this isn't working!', our recommendation is not to kill the experiment but rather to bring it up with your colleagues. Do they share your view? If they do, have a dialogue and listen to people share what they think you should do together. Often we don't see results or that it's working because we are still looking through the lens of the old leadership paradigm, which is totally natural.

How long does it take?

In our experience, this depends on the size of the organisation and to what degree the skills and mindset needed are present or able to be developed. With an organisation or team of up to thirty people, it usually doesn't take long before you begin to see results – perhaps eight or nine months. For larger organisations or teams, it can often take two or three years for the shift to happen and results to settle.

What about practices? Structures? Processes?

As mentioned in the introduction to this book, the third shift that Miki Kashtan emphasises is a structural one. We've consciously chosen not to go into detail here because there are lots of great resources that focus on that. Our focus has been to share what we've learnt about the mindset, leadership, and culture part of what supports organisational self-management.

However, we will briefly share the five core systems which Miki shared on the Leadermorphosis podcast. If you don't align these five core systems with the purpose and values of the organisation you wish to become, you will inherit systems from the previous culture, which is likely to undermine any efforts to becoming self-managing.

These five core systems are:

- **Decision-making system** (Who makes which decisions? Using what process? Who else is included? Who finds out about the result?)

- **Resource flow system** (Where do the resources come from and how do they get distributed? *i.e.* budgets, pay, human power etc.)
- **Information flow system** (How does information flow around the system?)
- **Feedback loops** (How do we receive regular feedback information about the impact on others of our choices? Who gives feedback to whom, when, and for what specific purpose?)
- **Conflict engagement system** (What set of agreements does the group make about what to do when there's conflict? Do these agreements support learning and reinforce values?)[5]

Clarity and transparency around all of these systems is vital in order to ensure you align these systems with the kind of self-managing organisation you're trying to create. As with everything else we've covered in this book, it's about creating spaces for open and honest dialogues in order to surface agreements and solutions in the group.

Safe travels

We'll close this book, as we opened it, with a timeless quote from Lao Tzu's Tao Te Ching. In it, there is great wisdom about the pillars we've talked about in this book: a coaching leadership mindset, a focus on climate, and getting and giving away the mandate.

---

5   See also 'Aligning Systems with Purpose and Values' on the Center for Efficient Collaboration website http://efficientcollaboration.org/aligning-systems-with-purpose-and-values/

The wise leader does not intervene unnecessarily. The leader's presence is felt, but often the group runs itself ... The leader's personal state of consciousness creates a climate of openness... The leader who knows when to listen, when to act, and when to withdraw can work effectively with nearly anyone ... To know how other people behave takes intelligence. To know myself takes wisdom ... It puzzles people at first, to see how little the able leader actually does, and yet how much gets done... Run an honest, open group ... It is more important to tell the simple, blunt truth than it is to say things that sound good.

Enjoy the journey!

Acknowledgements

Karin would like to thank ...

Ricardo Semler without whose books none of the stories in this book would have happened. Thank you for having been such a pioneer and inspiration to the world for decades. I'd also like to thank Bengt-Arne Svennberg who, when I came to TBV in 1989, shared and encouraged the idea of giving employees influence. In the rear mirror, I can see now how rare it was to think like that back then. I am grateful to Annika Tell at Freys and Lars-Åke Almkvist at Komanco, who were courageous enough to give me the opportunity to try those scary, new ideas with them in their organisations. I'd like to thank all my colleagues at Elisabethgården, Mötesbokarna, Svarta Siffror, and Underbar Hemtjänst for having faith, courage and patience during the years when we transformed the businesses together. Although not all the companies were mentioned and all the stories were told in this book, everything we endured and learnt together contributed. I want to especially acknowledge Jennie Forsberg and Ylva Franzén who in spite of countless setbacks never lost trust in this way of working. I owe great gratitude to all my partners at Tuff Leadership Training for risking their own money and also allowing me to invest Tuff's assets in acquiring companies together. David Valentin, Mette Herlitz and Eva Vilella in particular contributed many unpaid working hours for several years – thank you for your idealism and generosity. Thanks to Marlena Szajda for never ever complaining about the vast amount of paperwork and – not calculated – financial management occuring. Thank you also to early investors who helped us start up and especially fellow branch colleagues Pontus Holmgren and Jesper Höök for rescuing us in a critical phase. David Sundén became an invaluable advisor and business partner contributing his wisdom of business knowledge, and without it things would have turned out worse many times. I would like to thank all of you who read the manuscript and gave us feedback, you know who you are. And a special thank you to Joakim Manding Holm who spent a lot of time with it and gave brilliant input. Lisa Gill, thank you for joining Tuff and being my partner in writing this book, the work has been a true joy thanks to your magic with words, your in-depth knowledge and the quality of ease that is always there when collaborating with you. My partner in life and business life Carl Erik Herlitz; of course you get my greatest gratitude for always being open and stepping into adventurous projects which required major investments and hard work for us.

Lisa would like to thank ...

Carl Erik Herlitz, whose mentorship and wise, pedagogical ways have had a huge influence on this book and my own personal development. Frederic Laloux for writing Reinventing Organisations and teaching me about how to walk the talk – I have learned so much from you. Perry Timms whose generosity and encouragement was the catalyst I needed to do the work I'm doing today. Dunia Reverter for being the brilliant connector that brought Karin and I together in the first place and for your feedback on an early book draft.

Thank you so much to the wonderful, trusted advisors who gave feedback on various drafts including the gracious Helen Sanderson and the wise Susan Basterfield. I'm also grateful to Ants Cabraal whose support and jamming really contributed to this book and helped get it over the line. Thank you to people who've been inspirations and conversational sparring partners over the years like Kate Beecroft, Catalina Contoloru, Mark Eddleston, Jurriaan Kamer, Manuel Küblböck, Henri Lipmanowicz, Keith McCandless, Joost Minnaar, Simon Mont, Tom Nixon, Barry O'Kane, Francesca Pick, Samantha Slade, Horatiu Ticau and so many others. A huge thank you to all the guests on the Leadermorphosis podcast who've helped challenge and shape my thinking. And to my Shaun for being a constant support and Scouse cheerleader for everything I do.

Finally, thank you Karin for giving me the opportunity to co-author this book and step into your world. It's been a life-changing experience and I love every minute of our adventures together.

Recommended resources

BOOKS

Stories about self-managing organisations

Bakke, Dennis. *Joy at Work*, 2005
Blakeman, Chuck. *Why Employees Are Always a Bad Idea*, 2014
Getz, Isaac. *Freedom Inc: How Corporate Liberation Unleashes Employee Potential and Business Performance*, 2009
Kirkpatrick, Doug. *Beyond Empowerment: The Age of the Self-Managed Organization*, 2011
— *The No Limits Enterprise: Organizational Self-Management in the New World of Work*, 2019
Laloux, Frederic. *Reinventing Organizations*, 2014
Semler, Ricardo, *Maverick!*, 1993

On climate

Hamilton, Diane Musho. *Everything is Workable: A Zen Approach to Conflict Resolution*, 2013
Mindell, Arnold. *Sitting in the Fire: Large Group Transformation Using Conflict and Diversity*, 1995
Patton, Bruce; Stone, Douglas; and Heen, Sheila. *Difficult Conversations*, 1999
Scott, Susan. *Fierce Conversations: Achieving Success at Work & Life, One Conversation at a Time*, 2002

151

Switzler, Al; Grenny, Joseph; and McMillan, Ron. *Crucial Conversations: Tools for Talking When Stakes Are High*, 2002

On working in teams

Edmondson, Amy. *The Fearless Organization: Creating Psychological Safety in the Workplace for Learning, Innovation, and Growth*, 2018
— *Teaming: How Organizations Learn, Innovate, and Compete in the Knowledge Economy*, 2012
Fleming, Andy; Helsing, Deborah; Laskow Lahey, Lisa; Miller, Matthew L.; and Kegan, Robert. *An Everyone Culture*, 2016
Logan, Dave; and Zaffron, Steve. *The Three Laws of Performance: Rewriting the Future of Your Organization and Your Life*, 2009
McChrystal, General Stanley. *Team of Teams: New Rules of Engagement for a Complex World*, 2015
Schutz, Will. *The Human Element: Productivity, Self-Esteem, and the Bottom Line*, 1994
Wheelan, Susan. *Creating Effective Teams: A Guide for Members and Leaders*, 1999

On coaching

Tenelius, Karin. *Coaching Jobseekers*, 2010 (the jobseeker focus aside, this is a handbook for our method of coaching)
Whitworth, Laura; Kimsey-House, Henry; and Sandahl, Phil, *Co-Active Coaching: New Skills for Coaching People Toward Success in Work and Life*, 1998

On leadership

Block, Peter; and Koestenbaum, Peter; *Freedom and Accountability: Applying Philosophic Insight to the Real World*, 2001

Block, Peter. *Stewardship: Choosing Service Over Self-Interest*, 1993

Hagemann, Hans W. *The Leading Brain: Powerful Science-based Strategies for Achieving Peak Performance*, 2017

Kimsey-House, Karen and Henry. *Co-Active Leadership: Five Ways to Lead*, 2015

Marquet, David. *Turn the Ship Around*, 2012

Watkins, Alan. *4D Leadership: Competitive Advantage Through Vertical Leadership Development*, 2015

Wheatley, Margaret. *Leadership and the New Science*, 1992
— *Who Do We Choose To Be? Facing Reality, Claiming Leadership, Restoring Sanity*, 2017

Podcasts

Leadermorphosis – http://leadermorphosis.co

Team Human – http://teamhuman.fm

Work Life with Adam Grant – https://www.ted.com/podcasts/worklife

Videos

Frederic Laloux's 'Insights for the Journey' – https://thejourney.reinventingorganizations.com

Appendix

In Part 1, Chapter 1 we introduced the five cornerstones of a coaching mindset and way of being:

1. Relating to people's potential
2. Placing responsibility with the group
3. Clarifying and distinguishing
4. Being able to be with it
5. Not having your own (active) agenda

The table on the opposite page is to help you identify which of the cornerstones are your main development areas. Read the text and ask yourself: which pitfalls do I recognise the most? (Note: These are deliberately written to be a bit provocative!)

Cornerstone	Possible pitfall	Confront your pitfall	Exercises
Relating to potential	I have difficulty seeing people as competent. I judge people as incapable, instead of considering perhaps they are operating in adverse circumstances.	Confront your own arrogance towards others. Who gave you the right to decide what people can and can't do? Reflect on the fact that strengths and competencies have different modes of expression.	Make a list of three people you don't have confidence in and describe each one in terms of their abilities.
Responsibility in the right lap	I don't want to risk getting bad results, so I compensate for the shortcomings of others by taking responsibility for them and their work or development. I tell them what to do instead of releasing their own power.	Where in your own life do you take on responsibilities which are not yours? How would it look if you stopped trying to take responsibility for others? What does it cost you to take on others' responsibilities? What stops you from letting go of responsibilities that aren't yours?	Experiment with being excessively irresponsible for a period of time! Let a situation break down by refusing to take responsibility and notice what happens. Be concrete about how and where you will do this.
Clarifying and summarising	I like my own ideas and solutions, so encourage a passive mood when people come to me for support. I'd like to be able to accept the suggestions of others, but I'm so focused on my own ideas I often don't hear what they're saying.	Who wants to know what you think? What are your views really worth? You are robbing people of their creativity and desired outcomes. You make them dependent on your ideas and solutions, and in the long run, on you. You aren't interested in others and you talk too much!	Listen to people's ideas. Ask: 'What do you think?' twenty times a week. Choose to be quiet in a meeting and only listen. Note down what you hear.
Being able to be with it	I think that people should be 'better.' If they would only sharpen their ideas and pull themselves together, everything would be great.	Confront the idea that you believe you have a monopoly on the truth and if others don't agree with you, they're wrong. Consider that how you are being is actually working against how others are being instead of working with what is.	Practice acceptance. Identify three things you don't accept and learn to accept them.
Not having your own (active) agenda	I expect all conversations to lead to a specific outcome predetermined by me.	You can't empower anyone if you don't accept their aims and solutions.	Find opportunities to stop planning ahead and drawing up strategies. Go into conversations and meetings unprepared and ask, 'What do you need?' Connect with their agenda. Clarify their aims.

Figure 1: A coaching mindset and way of being – cornerstones and pitfalls

In figure 2 you'll find a simple assessment to help you determine the current state of your team both above and below the surface. You can use it as a starting point for your journey towards self-management, either by yourself or with your team, and to identify development areas. You can come back to it at certain intervals as you progress (for example, once a quarter or twice a year).

For each area, circle a number from 1 (low) to 6 (high) based on where you would place your team.

Low	Leadership	High
There is either a leadership vacuum, or one or a few people tend to lead in a parent-child way.	1 2 3 4 5 6	Leadership is distributed with individuals stepping up when they notice a need in the team. The leadership style is coaching and adult-adult. Leaders know when to step back.

Low	Climate	High
People don't trust each other, are polite, cautious, guarded, listen superficially to each other, are afraid to be criticised or to criticise. There are unspoken moose heads everywhere!	1 2 3 4 5 6	Colleagues trust and respect each other, share their opinions and needs, and can talk about what's in the way for collaboration above and below the surface. Moose heads are carried out regularly.

Low	Mandate and involvement	High
Only a few people are able to influence business outcomes. Most are either passive or feel they don't have permission to change things.	1 2 3 4 5 6	There are clear agreements about the mandate and authority of leaders, individuals and different teams or working groups. Everyone has a shared responsibility for the business.

Low	Meeting participation	High
Some dominate, others are passive, some are ignored, people tend to talk at the same time.	1 2 3 4 5 6	Participation is distributed, and everyone is heard and taken seriously. The team pays attention to what is going on above and below the surface.

Low	Decisions	High
Decisions are made in an ad hoc fashion. They are either open discussions that drag on or taken without the knowledge or involvement of all those affected or with relevant expertise. Decisions are often disregarded when taken.	1 2 3 4 5 6	The team agrees which decision methods are best for which decisions and who should be involved, disagreements are welcomed and used to improve decisions. Everyone commits to decisions made.

Low	Transparency	High
Certain types of information are held by a few people and others are in the dark, or information is hard to find, access or make sense of.	1 2 3 4 5 6	People know where to find information about the company's finances and are able to make sense of the figures. All other information is shared transparently and accessible to everyone.

Figure 2: What's the current state of your team?

The following four questions are useful temperature checks for individuals and are four areas that profoundly affect whether people have a mental ownership of their work and the business.

You can agree together what frequency might be useful for answering these questions and what you do with the data. It's often a good conversation starter.

Satisfaction

This is about your satisfaction with the tasks and responsibilities of your role, and the physical or organisational tools you have to do your work.

Question: To what extent are you satisfied with your work?

Low   1   2   3   4   5   6   High

Engagement

Your engagement in your role will naturally ebb and flow. Putting aside particularly good and bad days, think about your level of engagement generally.

Question: To what extent do you feel engaged in your role?

Low   1   2   3   4   5   6   High

Meaningfulness

Meaningfulness normally comes from having clear objectives and a connection to your organisation's purpose and the part you play in it.

Question: To what extent do you feel your work is meaningful?

Low   1   2   3   4   5   6   High

Development

Being good at what you do and having opportunities to develop – both as a professional and as a human being – are important motivators.

Question: To what extent do you feel you are able to develop at work?

Low   1   2   3   4   5   6   High

About the authors

Karin Tenelius

Studying marketing in my twenties, I was inspired by Ricardo Semler and became interested in alternatives to hierarchical leadership styles. In 1999, I was given an opportunity to put these ideas into practice and I began a phase of experimentation.

Astonished by the power and capacity that was awakened in the employees, I saw how effective this way of working is and what incredible results it can generate. I discovered that using this approach to leading and organising, it was possible to turn around several businesses in deep financial trouble in a short time.

In 2003, I co-founded Tuff Leadership Training to provide training in the skills needed for managers to succeed if they wanted to lead in a more involving way. I also began to acquire and build more businesses in other sectors, running them in this employee-driven way.

Today, what excites me is growing Tuff Leadership Training

in Europe and beyond, as well as spreading these ideas further to people in all aspects of society. I live outside Stockholm with my husband and two sons.

Lisa Gill

Although born in the UK, I lived in Southeast Asia until the age of 18. After completing a Drama degree in 2008, my early career was a patchwork quilt of different jobs in different industries. Eventually I fell into Learning and Development and it was here I became interested in leadership and organisational development.

Drawn to more radical ideas of decentralised organisations, I left the corporate world and began working as a coach and consultant under the company name Reimaginaire, supporting teams and organisations that were interested in new ways of working.

In 2016, I met Karin Tenelius and began writing this book. After falling in love with Tuff Leadership Training, I became a Tuff trainer and now lead courses around the world. The rest of my time is spent as an organisational self-management coach either by myself or as an associate of Greaterthan. I was included in the Thinkers50 Radar 2020 list for my work as the host of the Leadermorphosis podcast and as a writer sharing stories and examples of self-managing organisations. Currently I live in Barcelona with my partner Shaun.